MW01616222

A Vision of Kingdom Christianity

A Vision of Kingdom Christianity:
Finding the Big Picture of God's Design for His People

© 2015 by David Robertson

Permission is granted to make copies of entire chapters or sections for use in group discussions, tract distribution, or for any other noncommercial purpose that brings glory to God and advances the message of the kingdom shared in this book. Permission is also granted to create study guides for local church use and to use the material and outlines for teaching purposes. Please contact the publisher before modifying this material or distributing it electronically.

1st Printing

ISBN: 978-0-9940501-0-6

Layout and cover design: Luke Flory

All cover and editorial photos obtained from Shutterstock.com
Cover photo credits—Foreground mountian scene: Rudy Balasko, Background mountain: Mikadun, Hand tearing paper: fotohunter; Interior pages photo/image credits—Cloud layer chapters: f9photos, Seeds: EM arts, Sidebar pillars: Gts, Pillar chapters: Brandon Bourdages

Printed in the United States of America

Published by:
Kingdom Vision Books
Box 62 Niverville, Manitoba
CANADA R0A 1E0

For additional copies, or bulk discounts for individuals, churches, and retailers contact:
www.kingdomvisionbooks.com
kingdomvisionbooks@emypeople.net
604 S Bond St., Bluffton, IN 46714

A Vision of Kingdom Christianity

*Finding the Big Picture of God's
Design for His People*

DAVID ROBERTSON

Dedication

To my dear brothers and sisters who have been part of four little churches in Manitoba, Canada: *Don't forget that God came. Fourteen years ago He met us in crowded living rooms, old graveyards, big tents, baptismal waters, stuffy town halls, and serious Bible schools. He met us in our great need. Don't forget the miles we traveled to be together and to be with Him. Don't forget that we started with nothing, and knew nothing—but God was there. We began with the desire for godly homes, for truth, and with a burden for our loved ones—don't forget. Don't forget the mistakes we have made; God met us there, too. Don't forget that God came and He is not done with us yet. I dedicate this book to you and to your children and grandchildren with the prayer that they will meet the God you chose to follow.*

To my low German friends across Western Canada and in Bolivia: *Your hunger for God's Word made preaching a delight. Follow Him.*

To brothers and sisters across the United States: *God opened doors of ministry and I came to you, but truly it was you who ministered to me in my need, and I thank you. Keep seeking His kingdom.*

To my family Laura, Jillian, Nicholas and Judy, Joshua, and Alexander: *You have been my closest companions and laborers on the way of the cross. I love you.*

Thanks to the many people who have sacrificed to help make this project possible. *Sometimes just one comment opened up a window of new ideas. I have been enriched by your suggestions, critiques, help, and encouragement. I count you as true fellow laborers.*

To men and women of every nation who dream of being a living expression of the people of God.

TABLE OF CONTENTS

FOREWARD

As a Christian teacher in the past, I sometimes introduced my high school Bible classes by asking the students to write their answer to this question:

"Why are you a Christian?"

Almost without exception, the students explained that "getting to heaven" was their main objective.

Now, nobody can dispute the importance of this objective. Yet it misses both the main objective of the Gospel and the primary theme of the entire Bible.

Jesus did not say, "Repent or you will not go to heaven."

He did say, "Repent for the kingdom of heaven is at hand [has arrived]" (Matthew 4:17).

So what is the difference? The first answer focuses on "me." It makes "my salvation" an end in itself. The result is a "save me" gospel, and Jesus said if a man seeks to save his life he will lose it (Mark 8:35). All around us we see the devastating fruit of this misguided "gospel"—individualism in all its selfish spiritual forms, with weak commitments, if any, to a local congregation of believers.

The second answer makes "my salvation" a means to the end God has desired since the Fall of man—a community of believers exhibiting to unbelievers what the whole world would look like if everybody obeyed the King. With Christ's kingdom goal, "my salvation" serves an end greater than myself—a "society of the redeemed" instead of my selfish lone attempt to attain heaven without a care about God's objective for my salvation here and now.

A kingdom is never just one individual. A person focused on a "save me" gospel is like an aspiring baseball player who never intends to join a team. No team, no game. The function of the team is the end of all the pitching, hitting, catching, and running. You can't play baseball by yourself. Likewise, Jesus made it clear from his opening statement that trying to be saved alone misses the point of the Gospel.

What is more, it misses the passion of Christ. Jesus never called the Gospel anything but the Gospel of the kingdom, not even once in all the Gospel record!

Immediately after His opening kingdom statement, "Jesus went about all Galilee, teaching in their synagogues, and preaching the gospel of the kingdom" (Matthew 4:21).

In the parable of the sower, Jesus identified the seed as the "word of the kingdom" (Matthew 13:19), and in the parable of the tares, He said the "good seed are the children of the kingdom" (Matthew 13:38).

The Lord's Prayer begins with "Thy kingdom come" followed by the best definition of the kingdom in Scripture: "Thy will be done in earth, as it is in heaven" (Matthew 6:10). The prayer contains the pronouns "our," "us," and "we;" not "I," "my," and "me." Clearly, Jesus teaches His followers to pray as part of a community, not as individualists selfishly seeking their own salvation without joining His kingdom as real members.

Finally, referring to the end of the Gospel age, Jesus said, "This gospel of the kingdom shall be preached in all the world for a witness unto all nations; and then shall the end come" (Matthew 24:14).

This striking focus on the kingdom of God in the teaching of Jesus cannot be lightly dismissed as incidental. Jesus did not choose His words carelessly. His exclusive use of the term "kingdom" to describe the Gospel must be taken seriously. The Apostle Paul clearly took it that way. He also made the kingdom of God central to his teaching. Paul certainly did not teach a kingdom with its high ethical standards "postponed" to a future dispensational era, as some false teachers of our day have wishfully imagined. He took up his Lord's kingdom banner of the Gospel for the present age.

At Ephesus, Paul entered the synagogue and for three months spoke boldly, "disputing and persuading the things concerning the kingdom of God" (Acts 19:8). Later, in taking leave of the Ephesian elders, he said, "I know that ye all, among whom I have gone preaching the kingdom of God, shall see my face no more" (Acts 20:25). At the end, "Paul ... received all that came in unto him, preaching the kingdom of God" (Acts 28:31).

This exclusive definition of the Gospel as the kingdom of God by both Jesus and Paul is so striking, I find myself amazed that it has been missed. Brother David Robertson has not missed it. He has caught this kingdom theme of the Gospel with all its breathtaking implications. He shows us the kingdom potential to showcase the glorious character of God before an unbelieving world. His discussion is full of fresh insight and practical realism.

Brother David teaches us how this lofty theme of the kingdom can be translated into real life with all its untidy human elements. He does not deftly sidestep the defeating human issues that have plagued the kingdom (currently, the church) throughout its history. Rather, he shows how this "messy humanness" can finally be resolved in honest obedience to the practical salvaging (salvation) powers of the Gospel. Through this inspiring, practical study, every reader can learn to practice his personal salvation as a means to its true end—the attractive kingdom society God originally intended for all people to see.

May this generation repent of its devastating "save me" individualism and rise up to realize local colonies of this kingdom in all its compelling glory throughout the whole world.

Rise up, O men of God!

Have done with lesser things;

Give heart and soul and mind and strength

To serve the King of kings.

Rise up, O men of God!

The church for you doth wait;

Her strength unequal to her task:

Rise up and make her great!

John D. Martin
Chambersburg, Pennsylvania
26 January 2014

FOUNDATIONS

Foundations are very important. A house with a poor foundation is sure to give countless problems and fall apart long before its time. Likewise, when we ignore or alter the foundations of the faith, the results are sure to be disastrous. A weak foundation can never support the beautiful building of our lives and Christ's church.

We may have great teaching on marriage, communication, biblical eldership, or specific books of the Bible, but if the foundational ABC's of the faith are not solidly in place, we will suffer loss. The problem is that most of us would rather renovate and redecorate the interior of the house. But if the foundation is what really needs to be strengthened, we must do that first—foundations are critically important.

We have all heard that the foundation is Christ, but this does not mean some fuzzy, abstract, indefinable Christ. The foundation is the life He actually lived and the kingdom He came to establish on the earth. Jesus laid the foundation of what we could fittingly call **kingdom Christianity**. He announced the arrival of God's kingdom, shared the specific message of that kingdom, started a living community of the kingdom, warned about the enemy of the kingdom, and called on us to go out as ambassadors to advance God's kingdom.

When the church goes through times of shaking and confusion it is important to stop renovating and redecorating the upper portions of our spiritual house, and to instead, take time corporately to examine the foundations. If they are faulty, our other efforts will indeed be short-lived.

As you read the pages that follow, you will see that I come from a background of *evangelical Protestant Christianity* and am moving towards the *kingdom Christianity* that characterized much of the early Anabaptist movement. Ironically, while I am moving one way, masses of Anabaptist people are moving the other way—toward the Protestantism that their fathers died for rejecting.

The Anabaptists, in their beginnings during the 1500s, had a view of Christianity that was *distinctly different* from that of the masses of Christendom around them. On the basis of these differences, they were forced to separate from the more popular Protestant Reformers. Clearly there were two significantly different understandings of what Christianity is and of how it is worked out in real life.

After five hundred years of separation there are some serious questions we must answer:

Was this difference justifiable?

Did the Anabaptists actually have good biblical grounds for their stand?

Do the concerns of the original Anabaptists still stand true today?

Is it still right and important to emphasize these distinctives and separate from the mainstream of popular evangelical Christianity?

So, does a difference still exist? Are there still two distinctly different understandings of the faith? I believe the answer is yes, and *that bringing positive, biblical clarity to that foundational difference can help us as Christians, as ministers, and as churches to follow Christ more faithfully and unapologetically.* I am not the only one who says yes to this question. A conservative Baptist church in our province has an annual Homeschool Convention, but they have refused to allow Anabaptists to set up booths because they consider the curriculum they offer to be in error. They see a different Gospel in the materials and have taken a stand.

Dad, mom, preacher, young person, do you understand the radically different and beautiful nature of the kingdom Christianity practiced by groups such as the early Anabaptists? Do you understand those pivotal differences well enough to make right choices for your future?

The Christianity of our age has been charting a course that is increasingly comfortable with the world. However, that world is plunging in an anti-Christ direction. All too often we in the sleeping church are being swept right along.

Blending with society is not going to help people find their way out of the ever-increasing darkness around us. Someone must bravely lead the way. *There must be a clear alternative that rejects the downward path of our world and calls whosoever will to come and follow Christ on a radically different path*—the path of kingdom Christianity. This path, we are told, is narrow, and few will find it, but those few will have an impact far beyond their small size. In the tiny seed of the kingdom is the beginning of what will be the largest herb in the garden (Matthew 13:31-32).

The major portion of this book is an attempt to paint a positive biblical picture of a kingdom Christianity that calls men and women to leave the world's direction and come follow Christ.

The Anabaptists of the 1500s boldly grasped the opportunity to chart a kingdom direction in the midst of the confusing and compromising Christianity of their day. Now a great and perhaps unequaled opportunity lies before us to seek to discover and live the life of the kingdom in our equally challenging and directionless days. To seize this opportunity and seek to live out God's design for life together will take more than a halfway commitment. Halfway Christians will miss the essence of true Christianity. That is why it is so important that we work hard to discern the correct foundation before we begin to build.

PART I

Something Is Missing: In Search of the Kingdom

"Then said Jesus unto them, When ye have lifted up the Son of man, then shall ye know that I am he, and that I do nothing of myself; but as my Father hath taught me, I speak these things. And he that sent me is with me: the Father hath not left me alone; for I do always those things that please him. John 8:28-29

"If Jesus credited His teaching and authority to His Father, then I too must see that my teaching is not my own but the Father's. Being His messenger means preaching His Word, not my ideas. The relationship of the Trinity is one of inter-dependence. They are always working together, not independently. Surely, then, I must be unashamedly dependent in all things."

So reads the inscription I wrote thirty-four years ago on the top inside cover of my first wide-margin Bible. That Bible is in tatters today. Only part of the cover sits on the desk beside me. Four Bibles besides it have been filled with notes and then fallen to pieces; but my original burning desire remains the same: like Jesus, I want to see what the Father is doing and do it, to hear what He is saying and say it; I want the same connection of intimate dependence that Jesus considered essential.

Beginnings

I was a newly married, twenty-year-old, borderline hippie with my heart set on buying an eight-hundred-acre wilderness ranch when my world got turned around. A head-to-head collision with a one-thousand pound steer in a corral at Lac La Hache, British Columbia launched me into a serious search for the kingdom of God. That day, I sailed twenty feet through the air, eventually landing in a hospital bed. While recovering from surgery, I began giving myself to the study of God's Word and prayer. My life changed, and God's clear call came to leave my passion for land and ranching behind, and to exchange them for a total commitment to kingdom ministry. I had no idea then where that new commitment would take me.

This commitment took me to years of door-to-door witnessing (the last thing I ever dreamed of doing), to four years in a Pentecostal Bible College, and then to eleven years of pastoring. But in all this, something was missing—that seriousness of *obeying Christ*. We met for "church" on Sunday and Wednesday; but what of the needy all around us? What of the young men and women I knew who needed so much more than two meetings a week if they were to survive and grow in the faith? What about the problems of my tongue, of anger, lust, materialism, and love of the world? What of the power struggles and hatred in the church? How could these things be? Why were there so many *words about the Bible*, but so little serious study and obedience to what it commanded? What of God's call to be a holy and separate people? And finally, what of the lost—and our barrenness in regard to missions?

I wanted to do what Jesus was doing and say what He was saying to the waiting world. But instead life and ministry seemed canopied under a great cloud. I was born and raised on "Readers Digest religion" in Canada's most liberal church. I had left that and my dream of ranching, but there had to be something more than what I was experiencing. Instead of us changing the church to be more like Christ and His Word, it was changing us to be more like the world! Eventually, Laura and I and our four children left the ministry and retreated to an isolated Rocky Mountain village. We wanted to set aside a couple of years to seek God and ask specifically what He intended the Christian life and the church to be. The two years turned into nine. They were years of de-programming (if I can put it that way) and re-programming. My time during those years was largely divided between time alone with God in a small retreat cabin, time working with my family, and time interacting with the conservative Mennonite people who surrounded us.

We never did join the Mennonite church, but our interaction with them caused me to go back to the Scriptures again and again to see what they really said. We have spent the last eleven years in Manitoba fellow-shipping with a loosely-connected group of churches often known as the Remnant or Charity movement. These have been tremendous years of ministry for the whole family, years of seeking to encourage people of Hutterite, low German, Amish, and homeschool backgrounds.

During each period of life, God has taught, inspired, and directed us as a family into steps of obedience and ministry. I have learned from my Protestant, evangelical, and Pentecostal brethren, but I finally have planted my feet in the stream of those groups who down through history have been seeking to restore and return to a biblical New Testament brotherhood, those who search for, and seek to live out the whole Word of God. This stream includes early monasticism and many other groups that have separated from both the Roman Catholic Church and the state churches of the Protestant Reformation (e.g., Waldensians, Unity of the Brethren, Anabaptists, Moravians, early Methodists, some Brethren groups, and many more). Many of these groups separated from churches that insisted on compromising Scripture to keep peace with the world system and its governments. They often separated at the risk of losing their lives for obeying God rather than man. These daring men and women often were bound together in strong supportive communities of faith (which, of course, is what God desires, but seldom is as vital as in times of persecution and mutual need). The bold witness and fellowship of these radical groups often had a great impact on the people around them.

I have chosen to refer to these groups from the past and from our day as *Radical Believer's Churches* or at times as *Anabaptists* because that is the group with which I am most familiar. By way of definition, *radical* means *root, most basic,* or *original*; *believers* implies that the church is made up only of true followers of Jesus—not of everyone who chooses to attend or was born into the church; *Anabaptists* means *re-baptizers* and referred originally to those in the 1500s who had been baptized as babies into the Catholic or Reformed Protestant churches and later were re-baptized as adults when they came to a personal saving faith in Christ. To varying degrees, these groups of radical believers sought to live out the vision of kingdom Christianity and rejected the temptation to adopt the popular Christianity that would appeal to the masses.

As you can see, we as a family have made some definite and thought-out changes in our direction. We have sought to be a faithful part of a people who have a fire burning within, to maintain a serious commitment to practical obedience that leads to godly families and fruitful lives, and to cultivate an openness toward and patience for the seekers and strugglers who come our way. All of this is a huge task, and we have experienced times of great blessing and growth as well as times of great failure. I still do not see or do just what the Father is doing. I miss so much. I still do not say only what He is saying, but, "forgetting those things which are behind, and reaching forth to those things which are before, I press toward the mark for the prize of the high calling of God in Christ Jesus." (Philippians 3:13-14).

I firmly believe that

- God still has a great purpose for His church.
- We have made steps toward discovering and fulfilling that purpose.
- We still are falling far short of His desire.
- Much land still is left to retake and giants left to kill; this will not just suddenly happen.
- It would be arrogant for any of us as individuals or churches to assume we have arrived.
- We must stop, evaluate, study, repent and "hear what the Spirit has to say to the churches" (Revelation 2-3).
- We must set our sights on the glorious spiritual mountain peaks, and, like Paul take the next obedient steps to press on toward the mark of higher ground.

Parables of the Lesser Kingdom

I love the crisp clarity of mountain peaks and blue skies; I rejoice even more when I get greater clarity into God's truth. In the remainder of this book I aim to give you a big, panoramic, many-sided view of the spiritual mountain range that God wants His children first to see, and then to set out to climb. This isn't as easy as it sounds, so first consider a couple of parables:

Imagine this scene:

> More than two hours from the little Rocky Mountain village where I lived was the largest city in the north. I am sure that there were good things about that place—it provided jobs, shopping, lumber, plywood, chipboard and paper—but what I remember it for was smog. We would arrive at the top of a hill with a long road descending into the valley, and there below us sat the pulp and paper mills billowing out their endless clouds of smoke and their obnoxious smells. Up on the hill, the sun could be shining, the sky blue with billowy white clouds, and the northern air pure, but down in the city you would not have known it—in fact, I think people down below just got used to life in the smog. They didn't know what they were missing up above.

Now think of another more positive imaginary scene:

> Travelers in Europe are driving under a canopy of cloud that hovers a thousand feet above them. They come to a sign announcing that they have just entered Switzerland, and, not knowing anything of the geography of the land, they begin to explore the cobblestone streets, admiring the interesting houses with their colorful shutters and window boxes, and enjoying the cathedrals, museums, quaint villages, rivers, and lakes. They notice some steep hills and curved roads, vaguely realizing that there must be something more to this

country, something missing, something that they cannot see, but they carry on, never knowing that they have missed seeing some of the world's most beautiful mountain scenery. The clouds had curtained off Switzerland's most spectacular glory.

In the first story, the people settle for life in the urban smog. In the second story, they see amazing sights; but in both stories, they miss seeing the beauty all around them. The underlying assumption of this whole book is that something is missing or distorted in much of modern church life. We—and that means you and me—have too often settled for a lesser vision of the kingdom of God. In fact, the glorious vision of that kingdom is many times blocked off and hidden from our sight by layers of man-made smog, individualism, disobedience, doubt, and wrong ideas. Let's be honest—we easily become used to this altered gospel, to a lesser kingdom, and to a partial vision of God's purposes. Praise God for the partial vision and experience, but partly right is also partly wrong, and I, for one, do not want to get comfortable with being partly wrong. I want to seek the full and glorious vision of His kingdom and His righteousness. I want to identify the hindering clouds and smog that we have manufactured and rise above them. I want to think seriously about the faith.

Thinking Seriously About the Faith

What you see and understand spiritually affects how you live. For instance, if you see God as a big policeman who loves to punish, life as ho-hum, and people as untrustworthy and out to get you, then your whole life will be influenced by that outlook. Likewise, if God is impersonal and far away and the rule of life is survival of the fittest, the scramble to get to the top, or the drive to make the most money, then your life will be directed accordingly. I am saying that your theology, (what you believe or don't believe about God and His purposes for man) will direct how you live and the kind of decisions you make.

The problem is that the average person inherits much of his belief and lifestyle from his or her family or school. In other words, it is not seriously thought through. That is why it is possible to go through life with limited spiritual vision under a canopy of smog or cloud and not even know what you are missing. You could say you have been cheated.

Let's admit that all of us are in some areas under a cloud of ignorance. We either don't know or don't act on what God has revealed as the truth for life. However, there are some major, essential pillars of the Christian faith that, if rightly understood, will lay a foundation for fruitful living and open up the heavens so that we can better understand God's purposes for all of life. Yes, we all will be ignorant or wrong in some things, but if we are wrong in the most basic and foundational things of the faith, we are in great trouble.

In what other area is it more likely that Satan will attack, distort, and seek to blind us, than in these foundational truths? The fact is that our theology (our beliefs relating to God and His purpose for man) may be right, or it may be wrong. The Bible is what pushes back the clouds and reveals the truths about God and life as He intended it, so we must go to the Bible for authoritative answers.

I want to suggest that Satan has indeed successfully attacked the basic foundational pillars of the faith, so it is critical that we engage in the serious and hard work of reevaluating what those most basic truths are and whether we truly believe them and want to live by them. Remember the people under the northern smog and the Swiss cloud? Both had partial reality, but what they did not see changed the whole picture. So, too, in our Christian life—we may be partly right, but what we do not see totally alters the picture.

I want to appeal to you. I said that ensuring that we have a strong foundation is hard work, and it is, but dad, mom, young person, pastor, it is *critical work*. So many people have helped shape my understanding of the foundational pillars that God has given to His church, but— please hear me—above all, my understanding of these pillars has grown out of my failures and the agony of seeing others trying to build with a faulty foundation. I hope these lessons, crystallized through my own deep failures and trials, can help you build a foundation in your church and home that will hold up the beautiful building God intends for generations to come.

MEMORY AID

- There have always been groups of radical believers—kingdom Christians.
- We tend to see only part of the Gospel or to miss important truths behind the smog.
- We need to have the basic foundational truths right, or the whole building is endangered.
- Satan will seek to distort or replace the most important and foundational truths.
- He has done this, so we need to seriously reevaluate the foundations.
- Foundation building is hard work, but its fruit will last for generations.

Looking Ahead...

In Part Two, we examine twelve of the basic pillars of the faith, but before we do so, I want to consider four problems that restrict our vision and create man-made cloud layers that alter the faith and keep us from seeing the big picture of God's kingdom:

1. An emphasis on the parts (individual doctrines) but missing the big picture

2. The attempt to make Anabaptism more Protestant

3. The temptation to separate spiritual experience and practical obedience

4. A focus on faith as an individual matter ("I believe") that neglects the importance of the corporate ("We believe")

What follows is important, but it may be hard work to understand. If it is, skip to Part Two and come back to it later.

CLOUD LAYER 1

The Big Picture Is Being Replaced by Little Pieces

If you are like me, you probably wonder, "What is God's purpose and will for my life?" That is a very important question, but the first step in answering that question is to ask, "What are God's grand design, purpose and commandments for all of life?" These form the big picture of the kingdom, of which our separate lives are a small part. Rightly understanding the faith opens our eyes to the simple and positive vision of all that God intends.

I am aware that many times we fail to see the forest because our focus is on the individual trees. We tend to separate Bible truths into little boxes and not see how they are connected as a whole. For instance, I have often heard Anabaptist women say that they were told to cover their heads but never told why. They do it because it is what has always been done. It is on the list of requirements. Others have taken individual doctrines such as the end times, Israel, spiritual gifts, assurance of salvation, modesty, plain living, or pacifism and made them the central subject of their faith.

The point here is that all these teachings are only parts and must not be disconnected from the larger vision of God's ultimate purpose. If we fail as a united community to understand the big picture of God's kingdom, we will end up with just a box full of individual pieces. We will dispute about which doctrinal pieces are the most important, and one by one the pieces will disappear. There is a big picture of God's kingdom and purpose, in which all these pieces are held together as one beautiful whole.

Many times over the years I have heard people talk about writing a "statement of faith" for their church. When I hear that phrase, the image that comes to my mind could be likened to an encyclopedia. It has specific articles that outline facts about individual topics, and although this is valuable, it misses the reality that the faith is a unity. Perhaps we could say that the faith is more like a story or a vision of all that God has purposed and of the laws and commands He has implemented to make it a reality. There is a place for a doctrinal encyclopedia, but the faith you and I live by is so much more than a list of facts. The faith inspires, sets direction, changes lives and societies. It is a statement of vision.

After I had shared some of the truths in this book over several years of Youth Bible School, one brother said, "For a long time, I couldn't figure out why you keep talking about these things, but now I see. I see how central they are. Keep preaching."

The things you will read here are so basic, yet a distracting multitude of pet doctrines clouds the bigger picture of God's intent. In light of this, my desire is:

- First, that more of you from Anabaptist backgrounds would truly see the beautiful, unified picture of the faith, for I believe Satan is trying his best to blind and confuse us.

- Second, that some of you who are not from an Anabaptist background could have the opportunity to look at Jesus and the faith through a different lens. I hope this will be encouraging and enriching for you.

- Third, to present this big picture of the Gospel to my brothers in the faith and ask, "Is the basic thrust of this book representative of what we believe and of what we must strengthen in these days, or am I in the wrong, and missing something vital?"

- Fourth, to offer a unified outline of the faith that can be used for teaching and discipling in the church and home.

It seems to me that if the thrust of what I have identified as the Radical (again this means *root, most basic, original*) Believers' Church or Anabaptist faith is a non-optional core of the Gospel, then we must in humility strengthen it, for I fear we are losing it. But on the other hand, if it is in error and not the core, then we need to admit that we and our radical forefathers have been wrong and return to the Protestant, Catholic, or Eastern Orthodox understandings of the faith.

CLOUD LAYER 2

Anabaptism Is Being Blended with Popular Protestantism

In the last 150 years, the Protestants have had a great influence on the Anabaptist people, so there has been a tendency to deemphasize the Anabaptist distinctive beliefs and instead to line up more with the popular Protestant viewpoints in order to be more accepted by society. However, in doing this, the very nature of Anabaptism has been changed and made unclear and cloudy. I believe the Protestant believers have many valuable truths at which we Anabaptists are failing, to our great loss. We must hear also what they have to say, but I believe they, in general, like the original Reformers of the 1500s, have missed the essential Gospel core. As we will see in our study, the Anabaptist-type groups and the Protestant-type groups have two distinctly different understandings—

- Of the Gospel
- Of the Kingdom of God
- Of Discipleship
- Of the Church

As a young believer and pastor, I had a deep desire to get back to the teachings of Jesus, but for fifteen years I failed to see these two different understandings of the faith. I tried to mix the radical teachings of Jesus with the methods and teachings of the popular Christianity all around me (more on this later). Some of you may be struggling because you are trying to mix these two different understandings, and you may not even know it.

Protestant Emphasis: Words and Revival

Words, words, words! If I preach the right words, I am a good preacher. If my congregation agrees with those words, they are good Christians. That was my analysis of my years of ministry in a Protestant church. Yes, I had grown. Yes, God was at work in spite of us. Yes, I loved the people. But if I had to find one word to sum up my observations of our Protestant weakness it would be *words*. I was sick of words and sick of sermons. I wanted living reality, and I knew it had to begin in me.

Two things characterize evangelical Protestantism (in general):

- Words: an emphasis on the individual pieces or statements of right doctrine and sermons that expound those doctrinal beliefs

—and—

- Personal experience: an emphasis on conversion and revival

Both of these emphases are needed, but when they are divorced from the expectation of a radical, obedient faith, they lead to a shallow Christianity with a focus on the individual's experience—often past experience—and on his mental assent to a list of facts about the faith.

Words

Since the time of the Reformation, the central focus of Protestantism has been preaching and the sermon. The church of the Reformation was that place where God's Word was preached, that place where the individual pieces of right doctrine were defined and upheld, with the main doctrine being justification by faith alone. More recently the American fundamentalist movement of the early 1900s emphasized the importance of such things as belief in the virgin birth, the inspiration of the Scriptures, and so on.

Both of these schools of thought had some valid and good doctrines, but there also was a problem with each of them. They both merely emphasized words, words in sermons, words in doctrinal lists, and words in lists of fundamental truths. They were head knowledge. Those who merely agreed with their statements were accepted. The problem was that often no serious change of life had occurred. The Reformers and fundamentalists were seeking to battle against the false doctrines of the Catholics and liberal churches respectively, but they were not as concerned about the false and ungodly behavior of the people who attended their own churches.

Personal Experience

A second emphasis of Protestant evangelicalism is experience—the experience of conversion, of revival, of a personal encounter with God. Revivalism began as a result of dead formalism in many churches in the 1700s; nearly everyone went to church in those days, but most carried on in their sins and had no personal relationship with God.

In the 1800s, revival came to the Anabaptist people in Russia and America through Protestant evangelists. The new burst of personal spiritual life and freedom tended to cause a reaction against a "works righteousness" practiced by the old church and also against "works of obedience" in general. So these evangelical revivalist movements have impacted the Anabaptist people of the 1800s and of today with both good and bad results—good in that new life comes to people who are churched but lost, but bad in that the tendency of the revived has been to be embarrassed about their background, their distinctive doctrines, their distinctive practices, and their identity as a group separated from society.

Anabaptist Emphasis: Obedience and Revival

Interestingly, the Anabaptist influence that swept across Europe in the 1500s was the revival movement of that time, but take note, its emphasis was that true revival would lead to obedience in all of life. The cry of the Anabaptists was that the revival and the doctrinal reforms of the new Protestant churches were too shallow and did not go far enough. The Protestant Reformers had separated from the Roman Catholic Church but were not willing to practice acts of obedience that would upset the people around them or separate them from the rest of society. They had what we today call a gospel of "easy believe-ism." The Anabaptist claim was that true revival will lead to a total change of life, to obedience to the commands of Christ regardless of the cost, and to a separate, distinctive, new society of believers.

For the Anabaptists, conversion and revival were just the beginning. They wanted to find the biblical picture of Christ and His kingdom and live it. Because of this dual emphasis of conversion and obedience, these men and women were condemned to death by the thousands by both the Catholic and the Protestant churches, but persecution did not stop the revival. It only fanned the flame.

CLOUD LAYER 3

Spirituality Is Being Separated from Practice

We Need Bones, Muscle, and Breath!

We need to realize that the flesh, the world, and the devil are trying their hardest to separate the spiritual life from the practical Christian life, that is, to separate inner spiritual experience from real, practical holiness. The flesh finds Christianity much easier if there is no expectation of obedience. The world lures us to fit in and not go against the flow, and the devil knows that if he can separate spirituality from practical holiness, our faith will be useless. So he convinces one group of people that obedience is legalism and that only "heart Christianity" counts, and then he convinces the other group that experience, emotion, evangelism, and life are bad and will lead people away from obedience. Thus, spirit and practice are seen as opposed to each other, and Christians choose to line up with either one camp or the other.

God's design is that spirituality and practical obedience go together. This unity of spirit and practice was the heart cry of Moses, the Old Testament prophets, Jesus, and the apostles. It was the original testimony of the revivals in the early church and among the Waldensians, the Bohemian Brethren, the Anabaptists, the Moravians, the early Methodists, the Salvation Army, the early Pentecostals, and other revival movements. But when revival came again to the Anabaptist people in the late 1800s and the 1900s, it caused an eventual reaction against practice and a resistance to any kind of identity or lifestyle that would separate the church from the world.

Because it was the Protestant churches that were bringing new life to the dry bones of many Anabaptists, some tended to think that the evangelical revivalists must have the truth (the core), and that the distinctive doctrines and practices of the Anabaptist and Radical Believers' Churches were just little extras, even optional extras, that could be discarded as so much old baggage. I am concerned that this cannot work out right. I believe in the revival that is happening. I believe in vital personal experience. These are the breath of life to all our bones, but we still need the bones.

The bones are to the body what the foundation is to a house. Without bones, the body would be like a floppy bean bag on the floor. In his vision of the valley filled with dry bones, Ezekiel prophesies, and dry bones are gathered and then covered with flesh (Ezekiel 37). But for the miracle that this was, it was not enough. There still was no life. Ezekiel had to prophesy again and call for the breath of life to come and fill those bodies.

Now stop and consider that valley again. What if the bones still lay dry and scattered all over the valley floor and the breath of life came blowing in? Not a single body would have been joined together and prepared to hold the spirit of life, so any life-giving breath would have remained an invisible wind.

You see, we need the bones and we need life. We need the practical life of faith and the deep, inner moving of the Spirit. We need revival and obedience—the same kind of obedience that upset the first century world as well as the Protestant and Catholic worlds of the 1500s.

I want to suggest that the distinctive beliefs of the Radical Believers' Church are not extras but rather form an essential core. They are the bones, so to speak, the foundational kingdom teachings, to which the muscle of practical application is to be added and the breath of life breathed in.

Some of us Anabaptists have reacted rightly against liberalism. We have emphasized the muscles (practical application) and the breath (new life in Christ) but have missed the skeleton of the kingdom teachings (values) on which the muscle is to be hung. The result can be a form of fundamentalism, with people adhering to a list of conservative fundamental doctrines and practices simply because the preacher or church says to do so, while missing the shape and beauty that the kingdom skeleton gives to the body.

On the other hand, I fear that in much of the revivalism coming to the less conservative Anabaptist circles, people have unwittingly begun to discard both the bones (the kingdom teachings of Jesus) and the muscle (practical obedience). Application of truth has been made a matter of individual personal conviction or preference instead of brotherhood agreement. People can disobey God and invent their own private interpretations to justify how they live and yet still be considered spiritual because they are vibrant witnesses or are popular. How can this be?

Many of us in Anabaptist groups have been influenced by Protestant thinking and methods, and we have, in a sense, been unconsciously bullied into a form of Christianity that focuses on confessing Protestant creedal statements of what we believe (in our head and with mere words) instead of living out the doctrine of Jesus in a life of obedience. Even some of our Anabaptist statements of faith tend to be written using a model that lists all the individual doctrines of the Protestant groups and then merely "tacks on" a few extra statements. Is it not time to rethink this?

Rethinking the Faith in Light of God's Big Kingdom Picture

The journey in the chapters ahead is an attempt to step outside the box borrowed from the Protestant statements of faith and to present the faith, not as a series of separate creedal statements, but as a unified vision of God's big picture. I propose that the distinctive doctrines (teachings) of the radical and Anabaptist believers are not extras—not just an appendix or add-ons—that we can simply discard if we choose, nor are they a negative list of restrictions to be enforced. Rather, they are central, vital, positive pillars of the faith for which multitudes in the past have firmly stood at the cost of their lives. They are, I propose, still central pillars, so if they are missed or not rightly understood, many of the other important individual doctrines and practices will not come out right.

A relevant statement of the faith is written in light of the times in which we live. We face current challenges to the faith that demand our specific watchfulness and sober response. As the early Anabaptists sought to find their way and work out a clear understanding of the faith, they wrote several different statements in attempts to clarify and proclaim their convictions. They particularly emphasized the practical aspects of the faith. For Jesus, for Paul, and for the early Anabaptists, the faith was ethical. That is, it related to how they actually lived their lives, to their behavior. They would have seen true faith and obedience as inseparable, for the one led to the other, with the fruit of obedience showing that true faith was at work.

This statement follows in this practical Anabaptist and Radical Believers' Church tradition. It assumes that Christ's followers (Christians) are a group called out of our modern society to follow Him, and thus it is those who actually follow Him in this life who are part of His church. Going to a hockey game does not make you a hockey player, nor does reading a book about hockey. You have to put on skates and at least start to play the game. In the same way, going to church and even knowing much about God does not make you a Christian. You have to take up your cross and follow Christ.

CLOUD LAYER 4

The Authority of the Bible and of the Church Is Being Replaced by the Authority of the Individual

Is There Still a Place for a "We"?

The twelve pillars that follow each begin with the words "We believe…" but who is the "we"? We live in a day of increasing individualism—individualism in biblical interpretation and individualism in application. In fact, it seems the individual is replacing the church, replacing the "we," and the authority of the individual is challenging even the authority of the Scriptures. The question then arises: Is there still a place for a "we"? If so, then who is the "we"? And what do "we" believe? Amid the confusion of doctrines and directions we see in our day, one brother said to another, "We are not going that way." The immediate response was, "Who is the 'we'?"

I have written these pages as part of a dialogue that I hope will lead to more discussion and strengthening of the "we," and of those things that are important if we are to have a good heritage to pass to the next generation.

Revival has come and is coming to much of the Anabaptist church, and for that we thank God. But if we fail to acknowledge and embrace our distinct kingdom identity as a separated people of God, our beliefs will be eroded, we will lose the central pillars of the faith, and we will have nothing to pass to our children—who will then have no reason to stay in our churches. I encourage you to consider seriously the twelve pillars that follow, to make them your own, to teach them, and to help advance the message of the kingdom to every town and village as Jesus and His disciples did.

MEMORY AID

- To understand God's truth and purposes it is important to see the big picture of kingdom Christianity and all that God intends and expects.
- The faith is ethical—it has to do with how I live and is not just a list of words or truths to which I agree.
- We need revival and obedience—the bones and the breath, the foundation and the building.
- Rightly understanding the faith is a corporate affair—it is the job of the whole church, not just the individual, the minister, or the scholar.

I reititerate, foundations are important—they are to the building what the skeleton is to the body. Likewise, there are foundational truths of the kingdom that must be solidly in place if we are to have a faith that endures to the end. The foundations of the faith are under constant attack, and it is critical that we understand that failure in the foundations endangers the whole building. It endangers our faith and that of generations to come.

Let us "…earnestly contend for the faith which was once delivered unto the saints" (Jude 1:3).

PART II

*Putting the Big
Picture Together:
Essential Pillars
of the Faith*

Seeds of the Faith

The faith stands as mighty pillars, solid and unchanging. It rises as glorious mountain peaks, but it began its work in me as little seeds.

Dad was a doctor, but he loved people, not money. He could have built a successful medical practice, but he chose to take his family to the mission field. Mom was a doctor's wife, but she shopped at the thrift store, in fact, at the cheapest one. Dad took us skiing occasionally, but skiing was not his passion. He had a motorboat and later a sailboat, but they were just boats. Dad's cars were just cars and his houses were old but solid. We were town people, but when I was sixteen, Dad found me a summer job on a dairy farm, and I learned to work.

Dad and Mom didn't teach me the pillars in this book. I learned them later, but little seeds were being planted. I didn't see those seeds, but God did.

So the faith is about glorious truths, about strong foundations, about mountains to climb and giants to conquer, but it is also very personal—it is about God's work in you and me.

Why Do We Exist?

A question seldom asked and rarely answered is the one we have already considered in earlier pages. It is a question of such seriousness that it ought to be the focus for all of life. We could phrase this question in various ways: Why am I here? Why did God create me? What is my part in His great plan? On what do I base how I actually live my life?

As men, women, families, and churches, we live below the standard that God designed and intended for us. There is a great gap between what the Bible says about God's purpose for man and how you and I actually live. I have caught just a little glimpse of God's majestic purpose for His people, and I long to narrow that gap.

I want to remind you once again that discovering why you exist is vitally related to a correct understanding of the larger purposes and plans of God. In other words, studying the twelve foundational pillars that follow is not an academic exercise. It is part of understanding why you are here. To drive this home, let me share a story.

Which Submarine and Which Church?

A huge World War II German U-boat (submarine) is on display in a Chicago museum. Visitors can learn the history, pay to tour it, and see how it operates. But, in fact, the U-boat is out of the water, out of the war, and has no crew except some museum guides and caretakers. That U-boat fulfills a purpose, but it is not the purpose its designers intended for it. It has missed its calling! There are two different kinds of U-boats: those in the water and those in the museum. The one kind fulfills its calling, and the other kind serves a totally different purpose.

Let us relate this to you and me and the church. Many of us as Christians and churches have missed our calling. We are like the guides, teachers, caretakers, money collectors, and spectators in the museum, but God has called us to come and join His crew, the church, and to engage in a very real battle for His kingdom.

The devastating truth is that many of us who have joined God's crew have not yet graduated from basic training. We sit week after week listening to stirring messages, but have never been gripped by the eternal realities for which we as men and women exist. We have not entered into the action, and the horrible thing is that some of us do not know that anything is wrong. We are content to be in the museum! Our preachers, too, eventually become used to life in the museum. They begin to think they have been called to preach nice sermons and solve problems. The eye that once gleamed with fire becomes cloudy and dim.

How can this be? I, for one, cannot accept it. I cannot be content. I cannot settle for less, for I have read the directions—God's directions. The great need of the hour is for a company of Jesus' true followers to rise up in what has been called "holy discontent"—to ask the serious questions, read the directions, and then enter into obedient action.

I believe in God's crew, the church. I believe she is the most important institution in the world today. I believe she has been given the most important job on earth. I believe that the church of Jesus Christ will triumph. This victorious church is not a building on the corner. It does not consist of singing, preaching, or holy days. It is not a club to meet our needs, nor a group that believes a list or statement of certain facts about God. It is certainly not a museum piece! So what is it? To answer that, we need to go to the directions.

In the next few pages, I share some biblical answers to the following questions:

- Why does the church exist?
- What does she believe?
- What is she supposed to be doing?
- What does God intend her to be?
- Why are we so different?

We could call this a statement of faith, a vision statement, or a job description. Really, it is more than just a simple statement. It is an address to the nation—the Christian nation. It is a rallying call for us to gather together and take our place on God's boat. I am writing this statement as if you were the crew on the U-boat getting a pep talk before going into battle. The important thing for you as the crew to know would not be how the metal in the boat was made or how tight the bolts are, but rather, what is expected of you by your captain, what are the best ways to operate in the dangerous waters, and what is the great cause for which you are fighting. You and I, as Christians, could discuss many interesting but secondary topics concerning God and our faith, but most important: How is my faith in God to be worked out in real life? How am I to live? In other words, what is it that God expects of me if I am to be on His crew and engaged in the battle?

You may have noticed that I began with questions such as, "Why do I exist?" And moved on to ask, "Why does the church exist?" This is not a mistake. These questions must go together. The man who desires to follow Christ is called to join His crew. No submarine can succeed with a crew of one, and the same is true of the work God has for you.

The twelve pillars that follow are designed to help you better understand the big picture of God's purpose so that you can find your place in it.

MEMORY AID

- The church is God's crew.

- She is called to do His will.

- Each of us can discover God's will for our life, but first we must be committed to His greater purpose.

Seeds of the Faith—Pillar 1

The faith stands as mighty pillars, solid and unchanging. It rises as glorious mountain peaks, but it began its work in me as little seeds.

When I think of youth gatherings, I don't think of volleyball or guitars or silliness. I think of prayer and the presence of God.

As a young teen in the days of the "Jesus People," my parents took our family to Camp Farthest Out for Christ (CFO). The heartbeat of those camps seemed to be that God was involved in all of life. We spent hours being taught and singing. There were times of quiet, of writing, of drawing, and of sharing, and then, there was prayer. For two hours each afternoon little groups of people, ages fifteen to ninety, gathered to share their needs and pray for each other. When the day was over for the older people, the youth gathered in a circle for more hours of teaching, singing, and praying for each other.

It was there at CFO that I discovered that God is real. He is not just in church. He is here as we pray for one another. I was just a confused teenager with little teaching, but God came and met me and ministered to my deep inner longings. I came to know Him—I got my first taste of communion with a God who wanted to know me.

In those years, God planted a seed—a craving for Him, for the spiritual, for meaning, and for reality. Years later, that little boy, now a man with four children, still had that craving. On cold winter nights he would put on coveralls and head to the barn with a little light, a blanket, and the book of Psalms. He sang those Psalms, prayed those Psalms, wept through those Psalms, and met with God.

Knowing God is not just a doctrine—He is real, He is everything, and He wants to be known.

PILLAR 1

God Exists

We believe that God exists. He is before all and over all. He is the center of all of life. He is ever present and desires intimate communion with His people.

We believe that God exists, but who is He? How would we describe Him? Let's start with a different question. How would you want to be described? For instance, how would you like it if you were known as "Mr. Muscles"? There is nothing wrong with having muscles, but is it really what you want to be known for? Does it truly explain who you are and what makes you tick? I hope not. So what about God? How would He want to be described? What can we say about Him that reveals who He really is and what He wants to be known for?

In the Beginning...GOD

The very first words in the Bible are, "In the beginning GOD." "In the beginning God created the heavens and the earth" (Genesis 1:1). He was there in the beginning. To Moses He revealed His name, Jehovah, which means the God who is, who exists, who lives, and who always has lived! (Exodus 6:1-3).

Of this God the psalmist calls out in Psalm 95:

> *"Oh come, let us* [together as His people]
> *worship and bow down;*
> *let us kneel before the Lord our maker* [our designer].

[For, note these four important things that we enlarge on later]:

1. *He is our God…*   [Communion]
2. *We are the people of His pasture…*   [Community]
3. *Today if you hear His voice…*   [Communication]
4. *Harden not your heart."*   [Commitment]

Again the psalmist calls you and me to—

> *"Exalt the Lord our God and worship at his holy hill for*
> *the Lord our God is holy* [is separate]*"* (Psalm 99:9).

Our lives are to be lived as a daily response to God. They are to exalt, glorify, and honor Him. Our hearts are to overflow in worship because God is not just above all. He is here! He is present; He is intimate; and He wants to be known—He wants **communion** with us. That is, He wants a common union, a fellowship, a koinonia of deep sharing.

Our God is not far away. He is relational. In fact, the crown of His creation is not mountains or birds or flowers, it is man. He created the whole earth to be the home of His own people—a **community** to whom He is the Father and God.

Our lists of doctrines tell us that God is omnipotent (all powerful), omniscient (all knowing), and transcendent (beyond all). All of that is true, but with all those big words do we miss the simple thing that is closest to His heart—His love for people, His longing to have a people who freely choose to return His love? These two words, **communion** and **community**, show us something of the real heart of God. They show us who God is and what He wants.

When I was about twenty-two years old and studying the Old Testament, I read that the words **communion** and **community** could sum up the message of the Old Testament and the heart of God for His people. I have never forgotten that, and I believe it is true. He wants a people joined in true community who know Him and commune with Him. That is our God!

> *"Know ye that the Lord, He is God; it is He that has made us and not we ourselves, we are His people, and the sheep of His pasture"* (Psalm 100:3).

This idea of *knowing* is the same word used to speak of the deep and intimate relationship of a man and woman in a loving marriage. Repeatedly in the Old Testament, God says, "You shall know me" and know that you are my people (e.g., Exodus 6:7; Ezekiel 34:30-31; Hosea 2:20). Knowing is experiential and very personal. It envisions a God who is involved in our lives. In Exodus, after God had given Moses all of His Laws and expectations, Moses said, in essence, "God, I will not take one single step in following you and leading this people unless your presence goes with us." God, as a sign to be remembered forever, came down,

Consequences
of Ignoring Pillar 1:

Results of fear and ignorance of the Spirit:

- *Our church lifts up a high standard, but we are powerless to live it.*
- *We feel bound up by failure, condemnation, and guilt.*
- *Our ministers preach and lead in their own strength and we go to sleep or accuse them of being pushy dictators.*
- *Our people are captivated by worldly spirits and a counterfeit spirituality.*
- *Our life is dull and church life is mechanical.*

Results of life without communion:

- *God seems distant and unknowable.*
- *I am alone.*
- *I live my life like everyone else and add God on.*
- *My Christianity is just facts I believe, not life and vitality.*
- *I go to church, but my mind and life are not full of Christ.*
- *I have lost the sense of His presence.*
- *I have no strength or joy for discipling my children.*
- *My life seems purposeless and impossible.*
- *I give up.*

hid Moses in the cleft of a rock, covered Moses' face with His hand, and allowed Moses to see His back as He passed. He promised Moses, "My presence shall go with thee and I will give thee rest" (Exodus 33:14).

In the Old Testament accounts of this God we clearly see:

- The **Centrality** of God—He exists and He is ever present and central to all that happens in life and in history. *This is still true. Our God has not changed. What confidence we can have!*

- The **Communion** He desires—He longs to be known and to have rich communion with a people, who are recognized by all as His possession. *We have the fulfillment of all of this!*

- The **Community** He insists on—His people are to have solidarity. That is, they are to be one solid group, all united in Him and with one another. *This community is to be greater now than in Old Testament times, not less!*

- The **Communication** with God—He is the God who speaks and we must listen. He is not just a God that spoke in times past; *He speaks today through His Son and through His Spirit!*

- The **Commitment** He expects—absolute commitment, loyalty, and obedience are the condition. Anything else is spiritual adultery and will destroy communion with God, and ultimately the whole Jewish nation. *Once again, the New Testament takes this commitment to a higher level and calls us to take up our cross and follow on a road that few will find.*

Later we see more of this **community**, more of the God who speaks, more of **commitment** and of holiness, but it is important to see from the beginning that *these things are rooted in the very nature of God.* When we have truly seen the father heart of God for **communion** and **community**, it will only be natural to fulfill the conditions of daily **communication** and **commitment** (see again Psalm 95 above).

In the Beginning Was the Word

As we move to the New Testament, the central figure becomes THE LORD JESUS CHRIST, the Son of God, who, in fact, is revealed to *be* God. Here again, we are taken back to the time before creation:

*"In the beginning was the **Word**, and the **Word** was with God and*

The Word was God… He *was in the world, and the world was made through* ***Him*** *and without* ***Him*** *nothing was made that was made… and the* ***Word*** *became flesh and dwelt among us, and we beheld* ***His*** *glory, glory as of the only begotten of the Father, full of grace and truth"* (John 1:1, 2, 14, paraphrased).

All these highlighted words refer to Jesus, the Christ, who is **God**, the Anointed One, the expected Messiah. The Christian finds throughout the Bible a clear witness that Jesus is God, who, amazingly, came as a man. The Christian confesses that "Jesus Christ has come in the flesh" (1 John 4:1-3).

Of Jesus, the Bible says,

> He *"is the image* [in human flesh]
> > *of the invisible God…*
> *by him were all things created… in heaven…*
> > *and in earth…*
> *all things were created by him, and for him;*
> *and He is before all things*
> *and by him all things consist"* (Colossians 1:15-17).

The Bible tells us that Jesus Himself is:

- The Door—He is the only door to the Father and to heaven (John 10:1-9).
- The Way—He is "the way, the truth and the life" (John 14:6).
- The Vine—The Christian's life is *in Him*. In fact, this union is so close that Jesus says, "I am the vine, and you are the branches. Apart from your connection with me, you cannot bear spiritual fruit" (John 15, paraphrased).
- The Head—Christ is revealed as the Head, and we, His church, as the body—(the body, of course, is useless apart from the head).
- The Groom—Marriage is used as a picture of the mystery of the relationship of the church (which is the bride) and the Lord Jesus (who is the groom) (Ephesians 5).

In Jesus, it is now possible to have an *intimate relationship* with God that fulfills all the longings He had in the Old Testament times. When we know Him, we know the Father (John 14:9).

As we read, we also learn that Jesus is:

- Our Lawgiver—He has given new commandments that fulfill and go beyond the old ones (Matthew 5:17-19; John 13:34-35).
- Our Commissioner—He has given us a new commission or assignment and with it the promise that His presence and power shall go with us to get the job done (Matthew 28:18-20).
- Our Goal—The Father says that in Him "All things in heaven and on earth are to be summed up [wrapped up, united, brought to a conclusion]" (Ephesians 1:10, paraphrased).
- Our Judge—He who is coming again to judge the living and the dead (1Peter 4:5).
- Our Everything—He is "the Alpha and Omega, **the beginning and the end**" (Revelation 1:8).

In the Present—The Promise of the Spirit (John 14:16)

God the Father was in the beginning. God the Son was in the beginning, and now in the present there is a new beginning. For you and me right now, Jesus has promised the personal presence of His Holy Spirit. It actually is better, He told His disciples, that He left them, for then, He said, "I will pray the Father, and He shall give you another Comforter, that He may abide *with you* forever" (John 14:16; 16:7).

Forty days after Jesus ascended to heaven, on the Day of Pentecost, the Holy Spirit was poured out, and the church was born—the "Community of the Spirit" as it is often called. It was the Spirit's presence coming down on the gathered believers that marked the supernatural character of this new beginning. The people of Jerusalem saw the evidence of His coming. They heard it, and they marveled (see the book of Acts). Jesus had gone, but His Spirit had come. The church was born, and His great cause was going forward through His followers.

The Holy Spirit is the revealer, the teacher, and the guide. Jesus said there was so much that He could not say in advance, but that the Holy Spirit would lead us and teach us all things.

The divine person of the Holy Spirit is also the power behind the whole mandate that Jesus left for His church to accomplish in His absence. He gave us a job to do, a mission to accomplish, and, a message of good news (the Gospel) to carry into the entire world before His return. It is God the Father who initiated this mission; it is the Lord Jesus Christ who came to save and bring in His kingdom; it is man who is the mouthpiece and does the leg work; but it is the Holy Spirit who is the active agent in all that happens. It is He who convicts of sin; making us see our guilt and need, and of righteousness, implanting a desire for God and godliness; and of judgment to come, bringing an earnestness to be ready (John 16:8-11). The Holy Spirit bestows spiritual gifts and callings so we can serve. He directs us to seeking souls and opens our eyes to what God is doing. He enables us to plan and act in spiritually strategic ways that bring down the enemy's strongholds and open up doors of opportunity into spiritually dark places.

Blessings
of Embracing Pillar 1:

Benefits of the promised Spirit:

- *Streams of living water are freely flowing in and through us.*
- *Our life and ministry are in the power and anointing of the Holy Spirit.*
- *Our preaching and teaching has power and authority that clearly comes from God.*
- *The book of Acts is still being written!*

Benefits of communion:

- *I know there is a God.*
- *He is personally involved in all of life.*
- *He is relational, so I can know and love Him.*
- *He is ever present, so I can meet with Him right now.*
- *Taking time in His presence makes all of life work better.*
- *In His presence I gain strength to disciple and teach my children.*
- *Because He made us in His image, as relational beings, we can know and love each other.*
- *Because He lives, I have life; because He has forgiven me, I can forgive others.*
- *He gives purpose and meaning to all of life now and eternally.*

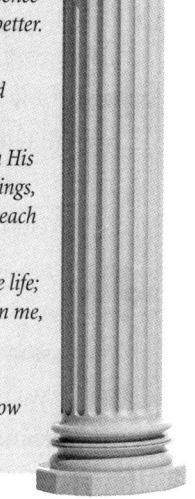

Before this outpouring on the church, the same enabling power of the Holy Spirit was publicly poured out on Jesus to initiate His three intensive years of ministry on earth (Luke 3:21-23; 4:1, 14, 18-19, 32, 36). Prior to that, we see the Spirit poured out on the prophets in the Old Testament. Everyone knew that God was in them, that God was working, that God was speaking through them. Now, the promise of God for the New Testament people is that the Spirit's outpouring is to be for all believers. All are to be filled. All are to prophesy. All are to be distinctively marked with power for living and service that is clearly not their own.

Our creed tells us we believe in the Holy Spirit, but we need to stop and remember that we are trying to go beyond the mere statement of words. We want to go on to actual life application and experience. So do you know the presence and power of the Holy Spirit in your life, ministry and church? Is it obvious to people who come to worship and fellowship with you that God is at work in your midst? If not, why not? Do you know His anointing? Do you even want to, or is it too scary?

We have the pattern of the working of the Spirit in the prophets, in Jesus, and in the book of Acts. We have the promise of that same pattern and outpouring for us. What a promise we have, but the sad story is that few have availed themselves of this supernatural promise and power. Down through church history many have preached, witnessed, and served out of duty, or from their own knowledge and burden. Many have served and spoken out of dryness and barrenness. Much good has been spoken, and much social action carried out in human power. But God said, *before you go*, you must be filled with power from on high (Luke 24:49; Acts 1:4-8). Mission ultimately is not the good that man does. It is *something God does* as we totally rely on Him: "Ye shall receive power after that the Holy Ghost comes upon you: and ye shall be witnesses" (Acts 1:8). The testimonies abound of men and women who initially served in their own power and then, out of desperation, found that baptism of power from God that inflamed and transformed their ministries.

God is at the Center of Everything

God the Father, God the Son, and God the Holy Spirit—the whole Bible is the record of their acts in history (His Story).

- He is the Creator and Sustainer of all things and all men.
- He is the King who reigns and has definite orders and rules for His creation.
- He is the Giver of new spiritual life to the Christian.
- He is the Head of the church, His body.
- He is the Goal of our mission on earth.
- He is the Power and Gift Giver that makes the mission possible.

You and I cannot sum up who God is. We can stand in awe and worship Him. People today worship many things. Some scream and yell and push through the crowds to meet a famous muscle man. They may get an autograph, a picture, or a handshake, but they don't know him, and he doesn't know them! I hope that you will push through to meet God—the God who is knowable.

Do you know Him? Have the clouds been rolled back? Have your eyes been opened? Have you caught a glimpse of who God is? Have you seen the heart of God for intimate communion? You can see a picture of this communion in the relationship between the Father, the Son, and the Holy Spirit, but it doesn't end there. It extends in the offer of rich fellowship to you. You can know Him! And that is so much more than shaking hands with a muscle man.

God Exists. He Is the Center of All of Life. He Is Present, Intimate, Before All, and Over All.

To believe this gives meaning and direction to all of life.

> *"To know Him, to know Him;*
> *Is the cry of my heart;*
> *Spirit reveal Him to me;*
> *To hear what He's saying,*

Gives strength to my bones;
To know Him, to know Him is life."

• •

Some Comment Regarding the Memory Aids Throughout this Book

Before we move to the second pillar, I want to clarify that my goal in writing is not that you remember every detail you read, but that you see the big picture of the faith. We have just explored the first of twelve pillars of this faith—of God's design for His people here on earth. Each succeeding pillar will build on the others and blend to form a picture. The Gospel picture we are painting is not made with paint and paint brushes, but with our words. I hope that when you have meditated on these pillars you will be better equipped to paint the whole Gospel picture with both your words and your life.

If you are to share this big picture of the faith with your children, your church, or an inquiring neighbor, you will need to know the parts and how they fit together. As a tool to help you remember this word picture so that you can paint it, I use twelve words that each begin with C and that correspond to each of the pillars. For instance, Pillar 1 is Communion. I want to encourage you to adopt these twelve words or come up with some of your own. When you say the word, try in your own words to express the basic concept of what that particular pillar is about. In the Memory Aid boxes, I review the concepts of each pillar in several different ways, hoping that you will understand the ideas presented and not just memorize the words.

What a joy it is to meditate on the faith and share it with others. Many times I have sat at a table with my tea growing cold while I write out words and pictures on a napkin to explain the faith to a friend. But before I can freely do that, I need to have a good grasp of the big picture.

Please note as well, that while I attempt to capture the heart and essence of each pillar with a "We believe" statement at the onset of each chapter, these are not intended to be a complete or polished statement of faith.

• •

Memory Aid

- Pillar 1—COMMUNION—**God exists**—The central thing that marks God's nature is His desire for intimate relationship with His people.
- Pillar 2—COMMUNICATION—**God has spoken**—If there is to be relationship, there must be two-way conversation.

Seeds of the Faith—Pillar 2

*The faith stands as mighty pillars, solid and unchanging. It rises as
glorious mountain peaks, but it began its work in me as little seeds.*

*At twenty years of age and married for almost two years, I had
enrolled in a four-year Bachelor of Theology program at a Pentecostal
Bible School. There was one problem. I didn't know what I believed,
or what they believed. In fact, I was so new to the church that I didn't
even realize they were opposed to smoking.*

*In class, I soon learned that there were different ways to consider
the message of the Bible. One method was systematic theology. This
method looked at the Bible topically. It created systems such as dis-
pensationalism in which to fit all the information. Somehow it didn't
seem right.*

*During year two, I was introduced to biblical theology. The idea here
was that God actually had a specific message to convey. My job as a
Bible reader was to find out the actual message that He intended to
communicate through each book of the Bible. Now that made sense.*

*I took up pen and paper, and as I read my Bible, I wrote out the mes-
sage in my own words. I outlined it. I summarized it, and then I took
more paper and started the process all over again. I didn't know what
Pentecostals believed, but I knew one thing. I seriously wanted to
know what God had to say, and I was committed to the hard work of
finding out. That desire was a little seed, and I had no idea then what
kind of plant was going to grow.*

PILLAR 2

God Has Spoken

We believe that God has revealed Himself. He has spoken and is speaking. His will can be known.

God has revealed Himself:

...in creation (Romans 1:19-25, 28)

...in history

...in the person and life of Jesus on earth (John 1:1-18)

...as Father, Son, and Holy Spirit

...as King, Shepherd, Provider, Healer, Guide

...in His Word

An Instruction Manual

The important thing here is that we are not left in the dark about God's will. *He has spoken. We can obey.* As we obey, more light shines on our path. As we obey, our life lines up more with His design. The result is that life works better, and we have more joy and fulfillment in doing what we were created to do. Someone has said, "When all else fails, read the directions." God has clearly given them to us.

Let me illustrate with something that happened to me this summer. A neighbor told us that if we could fix the knotter on her baler, we could use it for free to bale our hay. My son knew that I had some spare time and had worked with balers, so he brought it home. I worked on the adjustments to the knotting mechanism for a day. I thought that it wasn't working because one of the arms seemed to be welded at a 90-degree angle instead of a 45-degree angle, but I wasn't sure.

I finally found someone who had the same baler with an operator's manual, and went to examine it. All of that took more time and trips, but eventually I confirmed what was wrong, took the part off, got it heated, twisted it to 45 degrees, and got the baler working. We then baled five hundred bales with hardly any problems.

Once I found the manual and a pattern baler to examine, the actual repairs took only half an hour, but the whole process took almost two days. I am not a mechanic, but I had the mechanic's manual and a pattern. May I suggest that we also have a manual, the Creator's manual, and we have the pattern, the life of Jesus?

God has spoken, and because He has spoken, you and I do not need to guess what His will and commands are. Jesus said, "You shall know the truth, and the truth shall make you free" (John 8:32). This does not mean free to do as you please, but free because you are living in God's design, God's truth.

Truth does not come from you or from any other created man. It comes from outside of you. It comes from the Creator, God. What is made cannot instruct the Creator. That would make no sense. Rather, the Creator instructs us, and we submit joyfully with all our heart.

Hearing and Doing

In the Bible, Jesus said, "Whosoever *heareth* these sayings of mine and *doeth* them, I will liken him unto a wise man, which built his house upon a rock," and the storm beat upon that house but could not destroy it (Matthew 7:24-27; Mark 4:1-20). To the man caught up in himself, God's instructions make no sense. They are too hard, too costly. But just start obeying, start hearing and doing, and bit by bit you will grow in spiritual strength and you will have new inner confidence to face the storms and challenges of life.

Here is another illustration. Yesterday, we had a family with fourteen children, ages one to nineteen years, over for lunch. In one corner of the room was a basket of pine cones. On a low shelf was a bird's nest, and on the coffee table a display of fall leaves. When the family left, everything was untouched. The floor under the table had no spilled food, and there had been no behavior problems. Why? Because the parents had heard and heeded God's instructions for the family. It was hard work at first, but in the end, it made for easier work, and it bore fruit. So it is in a multitude of other areas. We begin to practice godly courtship, purity, thankfulness, turning the other cheek, and so on, and as we do, we find the blessing of God overflowing on our lives.

To hear God speak, serious believers have always turned especially to the commandments of Jesus and to the sermon He preached on a mountain (Matthew 5-7), in which

Consequences
of Ignoring Pillar 2:

Results of ignoring what God has already said:

- *I live as if there is no God; as if He has not spoken.*
- *My life and faith lack seriousness.*
- *I am really my own authority.*
- *I make decisions based on what I feel is right.*
- *Disobeying God's Word brings bad fruit in my life, but it's so dark now that I can't see it.*
- *My heart hardens and my thinking changes.*
- *I am on a slippery slope—I can't stop, and I don't even want to.*

He spoke of the requirements or laws of kingdom living. In this sermon we find teachings that seem ridiculous—about being poor and gentle in spirit, about expecting and accepting persecution, about what to do when people take things from us, about marriage and God's rejection of divorce, about prayer and forgiveness, about not storing up money or treasure, about worry, about judging ourselves, and about the narrow road to God that few find.

Jesus' teachings, the directions in His instruction manual, go against all that is natural in man. In fact, many Bible teachers try to say that Jesus did not really mean what He said. But take note, people in the early years of the church lived according to what He said, and they changed the world. They considered His teachings so important that thousands of believers died for them. They did not try to water them down or make them more appealing. As one man has said, we wouldn't even know of Jesus' existence today if what He said and lived hadn't been so radical that it shook the whole Roman Empire.

False Revelation (Not Under Law/Focus on My Feelings)

It sounds so easy to hear and then to do, to just follow the instructions. So why is it so hard to find a people who do this unashamedly? What traps and dangers have been set up to keep us from simple obedience?

The Bible warns us that in the last days great deceptions will come against God's people and against God's truth. Deception actually is false revelation posing as the truth.

One common, modern form of deception is a distortion of the teaching that we are free from law. "We are no longer under the law" is translated to mean that God's law has been abolished, so that there is no longer a list of dos and don'ts for the Christian.

Actually, Jesus said the opposite. He came to bring the law to its fulfillment. The law has been taken to a higher standard. The bar has not been lowered; It has been raised! In fact, the New Testament probably lists more ethical, behavioral commandments than we find in the Old Testament.

Another common deception emphasizes that God still speaks, which He does, but explains that what He (supposedly) says to me today is more valid than the absolute truths of the Bible. Much emphasis is put on what I am feeling or what I think I heard God say. It is often said, "I have no conviction about that," or "My conscience isn't bothering me." The problem with all these statements is that they imply that God didn't really mean what He said. They make man the one who decides what God means instead of accepting what the Bible says. What happens then is that those deceived in this way allow two kinds of truth: truth for me and truth for you. In doing this, they make "God" say different things to different people on different days because for them, there is no absolute truth.

I remember when I was a boy I had a little green man. I think he was called Gumby. I could twist and contort Gumby into any shape that I happened to feel like, because he had no bones. He was just rubber. Remember, we said earlier that the pillars of kingdom teaching form a skeleton which we flesh out making applications in all the specific issues and situations of daily life. Today we have many "Gumby Christians" who have replaced the kingdom skeleton with their own "spiritual" feelings.

Let us beware! God did not tell us that we will have warm fuzzy feelings to guide us, or that we need to feel convicted before we obey. But He clearly called us to hear and then act by faith on what He has written.

Now you may think that you are just not affected by either of these twists of the enemy, but let me share some examples. Have you ever been to a wedding at which the congregation was asked not to take pictures during the ceremony, but people went right ahead anyhow and took pictures? Somehow it didn't mean them or didn't mean just one picture. Now did those who took pictures just not have a conviction, or were they disobedient?

Or consider the employers who ask for no personal texting or emailing during working hours. Are the masses of employees who text and say, "My conscience doesn't bother me" stealing time from their employer? Are they serving him or themselves? Are they disobedient? They feel no guilt when they text, and so assume it is okay.

Now let me ask again—are there ways that you and I do this with God and His commands? Perhaps we read what the Bible says, but respond, "I feel no guilt," or "It couldn't mean what it says." Maybe we are putting Jesus' commands through a filter of what I *feel* is best for me.

Consider also the lady involved in an affair with someone who is not her husband. They love each other, and she believes that love comes from God. Moreover, she feels closer to God than ever before, so she reasons, "It can't be wrong."

Or think of the people who go to church weekly or on special occasions and get what I call a spiritual bath. They walk down the aisle on a plush red carpet. The light is shining through yellow windows, making the whole room seem golden. The great organ is piping out its majestic notes, and the soul is being bathed in warmth. You might say the sunlight is warming them, but no more light is shining on their path than before they entered. The same could be said about the feelings that come from going to a "Christian" concert, or even to a very rustic, plain service.

You see, my good feelings do not mean I am right with God. Revelation is not about what I think is right or about what I feel. *Revelation is what God has already said.* That is where I must begin. Instructions already have been given and *God means what He said!* If we get this, we are on the road to serious and joyful Christianity.

I often say that I have skied and climbed some of the world's great mountains; I have canoed thousands of miles of her incredible rivers; I have worked on one of the most beautiful of ranches: but that none of this comes anywhere close to the thrill and adventure of hearing, serving, and obeying the Lord Jesus Christ! So there are incredible blessings and fruitfulness if we choose to hear and obey, but what if we neglect these?

Do Not Add or Subtract

One of the most pointed warnings Jesus ever uttered stated, "Whosoever therefore shall break one of the least of these commandments and shall teach men so, he shall be called the least in the kingdom of heaven..." (Matthew 5:18-19). Teacher, beware! Dad, beware! The one who cuts out or changes what God has said and teaches others to disregard and disobey the commands of Christ is in grave danger. Scissors are not to be used on our Bibles.

Concerning itself, the Bible says, "Do not add to or subtract from the words I have commanded you, but keep them" (Deuteronomy 4:2; 12:32; Revelation 22:18, 19). Don't water them down or make them mean something else. "Keep therefore and do them for this is your wisdom and your understanding in the sight of the nations, which shall say ... surely this great nation is a wise and understanding people. Only take heed to thyself, and keep thy soul diligently, *lest thou forget* the things which thy eyes have seen, and lest they depart from thy heart...but teach them thy sons, and thy sons' sons" (Deuteronomy 4:1-9; see Deuteronomy 6:1-15; 1 Kings 22:8-23, 25; Nehemiah 1:5-9; Nehemiah 8:1-9:3; emphasis added).

> ### *Blessings*
> *of Embracing Pillar 2:*
>
> **Benefits of hearing what God has already said:**
>
> - *I know Someone bigger than me is behind everything, so I don't need to figure everything out.*
> - *I believe He has spoken, so I just need to take seriously what He has said and live it.*
> - *I believe there are absolute truths and authority that are to direct all of my life.*
> - *God has put a lot of thought into creation, and since I am made in His image as a thinker, I must put a lot of thought into how I live in His world.*
> - *I joyfully seek to apply God's Word.*
> - *Because I can see the fruit of it in me, I want to keep on hearing and doing.*

I recently read the sad account of a girl in Mississippi who was one of the first blacks to be hired in Woolworth's Department Store chain in the 1960s. One day she was being rude to an older black man in the store and he reminded her that the reason she had this job was because he and many others in the black community had worked very hard for the right to freedom and better jobs. He reminded her that in return, she ought to be grateful and kind to her people. Her quick response was that no one had done anything for her. She had been hired because she was qualified. It was only a few months since she had received this freedom and already she had *forgotten* those who had helped her. Her focus was now on herself. She thought that she was a "somebody."

One of the reasons we depart from a zealous faith is that we begin to think of ourselves as "somebodies." We forget how big God is; we forget what He has done; we neglect to teach and begin to feel we have been a little too serious in our desire to obey. Someone has said that forgetfulness and thanklessness are always some of the first steps toward departing from the faith.

This revealed Word of God is to be remembered continually. When it is accepted, believed, and acted on, it has power to work and to do what you and I could never do. It is "quick and powerful and sharper than any two-edged sword, piercing even to the dividing asunder of joints and marrow, and the thoughts and intents of the heart" (Hebrews 4:12). God says of it, "My word . . . shall not return unto me void, but it shall accomplish that which I please" (Isaiah 55:11). It is powerful to change lives, to instruct, and to reprove, in order "that the man of God may be perfect" (2 Timothy 3:15-17).

Finally, Jesus warns, "He that rejecteth me, and receiveth not my words, hath one that judgeth him; the word that I have spoken, the same shall judge him in the last day" (John 12:48). So, "Today if you will hear His voice, harden not your hearts" (Hebrews 4:7; also remember Psalm 95). The privilege of having **communion** with God involves **communication** with Him. And **communication** demands that you and I listen and respond with a **commitment** to act on what we have heard. The faith is not words we recite, but words we hear and obey. It sounds so simple, but it is the greatest challenge and adventure in life.

God Has Revealed Himself. He Has Spoken.

The more we come to know God's nature, acts, and Word, the more we will have light shining upon our path—light in the midst of the chaos and confusion of our modern Dark Ages. Someone must stand against the darkness. In the past, others have done it—will you? History is changed and impacted for God by those who hear God's unchanging instructions and begin to line all of life up with them.

Memory Aid

- Pillar 1—COMMUNION—**God exists**—The subject of the whole Bible is God's caring relationship with His people.

- Pillar 2—COMMUNICATION—**God has spoken**—He has shown us His will in creation, in the life His Son lived, in the teachings of Jesus and the apostles, and in the lessons of the Old Testament. We are without excuse.

- Pillar 3—COMMUNITY—**Peoplehood**—We will look more closely at the nature of the people who are called to hear and to obey.

Seeds of the Faith—Pillar 3

The faith stands as mighty pillars, solid and unchanging. It rises as glorious mountain peaks, but it began its work in me as little seeds.

The years after World War II were apparently dismal years for much of the American church. Man, science, and materialism were replacing God. Suddenly in the 1960s and 1970s the life of comfort was exploded with the advent of the hippies. It wasn't just the hippies that shattered the status quo. It seems that God broke in. People began seeking for the working of the very personal Holy Spirit in their lives. It was the decade before cell groups became popular, and before all the talk of spiritual gifts. It was the simple age of body ministry. Hungry, hurting, seeking, ordinary people gathered in circles after services, in camps, and in house meetings. They went around the circle and confessed their sins and needs. Then they took their place on the chair in the middle of the group while others prayed for them.

I was a teenager during those "body ministry" years, and I was impressed that this kind of caring was what God wanted His church to be like. I tasted a little part of God's heart for community.

Community isn't all prayer and body ministry. It's also living and working together. It's being deeply involved in each other's lives. Four years of boarding school (grades nine to twelve) introduced me to a tightly-knit society that was bigger than my own world, my television, or our anonymous family existence. St. John's was a disciplined Anglican school concerned with the 3Rs (reading, 'riting and 'rithmetic) and making men. The teachers were members of the Company of the Cross. They lived at the school, worked for one dollar a day, and were involved in all of life with us. The one hundred boys took care of all the kitchen work, cleaning, maintenance, and new construction projects. We also ran three businesses, and canoed, snowshoed, and dog-sledded thousands of miles together.

Western life is very compartmentalized, but for those four years I lived, worked, played, learned, and grew all with the same group of people. I learned something of the joys and potential of being united as a community with a common purpose. A few years later in my search of the Bible, I discovered God's desire for a people—for community; but the seed had already been planted.

PILLAR 3

Peoplehood

We believe God's design is to have a holy people who live in communion with Him and reflect the life and values of the kingdom of heaven. God's people exist to be communities of light in a darkening world.

Peoplehood or Individualism?

Consider with me for a moment. Is it actually *possible* for a people to live together in love in a world that is falling apart? Is it possible to demonstrate harmony, forgiveness, and forbearance, or do we, too, fall apart?

It seems that much of the modern church has concluded that living together in this kind of loving community is not possible and so *have changed their gospel*—changed it into an individual matter between a man and his God. The truth is that this kind of experience of community is humanly impossible—it is only the real Gospel that makes it possible.

Each of us must recognize our own disappointments and horrible failures in this area of church relationships. However, we dare not change God's Word to match up with our failures. His plan has not changed, so let us get up, dust ourselves off, make things right with God and man, and set our hearts to be that people whom He so much desires, or at least die trying.

God's desire for a **people** is not a secondary thing. It is a major part of His purpose from Genesis to Revelation. He is seeking *a* people, *a* body, *a* bride—in other words, a collection of individual parts united into *a* unit. If this is taken seriously, it upsets the individualism of our day. The focus in the Bible is not on *my* God, *my* salvation, *my* happiness, *my* ministry, *my* stuff, and so on. This focus on the individual and on *me* and *my* and *mine* is the man-focused religion of humanism. It is not Christianity. You and I are not doing God a favor by joining the church. God is not *my* special Lord whose mission is to bless *me*.

The faith, and a statement of that faith, must come against the false teachings and idols of our day. Certainly *individualism* and all its modern fruits are contrary to the heart of God. His desire is for peoplehood, for a living body to be expressed locally in literal communities of light in which we reflect the light and life of heaven. Much of modern life serves to isolate us and to make us self-sufficient and independent. If we are to be true to the faith, we must reexamine those things that hinder the building of intimate and intentional Christian communities.

At the birthday of the nation of Israel (Exodus 6:1-8), God made some promises:

1. I will bring you out from Egypt. I will redeem you. In other words, I will both save you *from* sin and the world, and save you *unto* myself (Conversion, deliverance, salvation).

2. I will take you for a **people** (Community).

3. I will be to you a God and you shall know me. (Communion—I am personal and knowable, not distant.)

He signed this covenant with His name JEHOVAH, which means, the God who is, the I AM, the Ever Living One.

Later, the Old Testament prophets, in the midst of Israel's backsliding, spoke of a future remnant who would return to God and become His people (Zechariah 8:6-8). Jeremiah and Ezekiel spoke of God making a new covenant with Israel and giving them a "new heart" and a "new spirit." He said that He would take out the stony heart… "and they shall

be my people, and I will be their God" (Jeremiah 24:7; 31:31-34; Ezekiel 11:13-23; 36:26-28). The book of Hebrews tells us that this promised new covenant has finally been put in place by the blood of Jesus and that God's laws have been put into the minds and hearts of those who put their faith in Jesus Christ. The result is a new Israel made up of believers of every possible nation who shall "**be to me a people**," and "I will be to them a God" (Hebrews 8:8-10; 10:16-26).

God created the earth to be a home for this people—a home for a **community** of men and women with no walls between Jew and Gentile, black and white, rich and poor, or employer and employee. The "eternal purpose which He purposed in Jesus Christ" is "to make all men see what is the fellowship of the mystery, which from the beginning of the world hath been hid in God" and *which is now to be made "known by the church"* (Ephesians 3:9-11, emphasis added).

God's plan has always been for a people who reflect His image, His will and show forth His many-colored wisdom and glory. He has always wanted a people who are fellowshipping with Him and with one another, and who together are managing "His farm"—the earth.

> ## *Consequences*
> ### *of Ignoring Pillar 3*:
>
> *Results of living without peoplehood:*
>
> - *Anonymous individuals gather to worship but are not a community.*
> - *Church is just one part of life, as are golf, work, and shopping.*
> - *Individuals relate to God without the involvement of their brothers and sisters.*
> - *I bear my own burdens.*
> - *When struggles come, bitterness and un-forgiveness grow.*
> - *When disaster strikes, the bank and restoration company help.*
> - *I give myself to some other form of society based on individualism, independence, materialism, power, or pleasure.*
> - *We have a club, but not a united, new society.*

God has been committed to this purpose for more than six thousand years, and He hasn't changed His mind. He began with Adam; then again with Noah; then with Abraham and just one select nation, Israel, who was to be a model of all He intended. Now in His Son, He has begun a fourth time in the church—a people to whom He has given His own Spirit *to make the job possible* (book of Acts). The unity and pure fellowship that God has always intended is to be made known by the church to the watching world.

So you see, becoming God's people, His community, is no small thing. It is important. It is at the center of God's design. Christian living is not just about my own salvation, attending church, or doing some witnessing. In the book of Acts we read the testimony of a whole new people—a new nation that together, as a unit, turned the world upside down as they lived a new life and culture that amazed everyone.

Sojourners and Strangers

The Apostle Peter instructs us about the nature of this new people, the church. They are to be holy (which means set apart or separate), "for I am holy," says the Lord (1 Peter 2:16). He says in the next verse that God's people are to pass their time on earth as sojourners—as foreigners, strangers, or aliens who are just passing through but do not belong here (1 Peter 1:1,17; 2:11; Hebrews 11:13-16; 13:14). Peter goes on to speak of God's new covenant people as:

• A Chosen Generation—a whole new race of people

• A Royal Priesthood—connected to God

• A Holy Nation—a nation within other nations

• A Peculiar People—who show forth the praises of God

Observations

Let me make a few observations about what it means to be His separate people:

1. First, it is clear that *a whole new people group*, race, or nation has been formed, not on geographic lines, but on a spiritual basis. Like every other people group, this new race will have distinctive qualities and culture. In fact, the qualities of this group are to astound those around them and draw them to God.

2. Secondly, *the new people are to be holy and separate* from all other peoples and lifestyles. They are *a replacement people*, for membership in every other nation and people group is voluntarily replaced with a new living membership in the community of the kingdom. Paul, in Romans 12:2, speaks of this separation as being "not conformed to this world," but rather transformed in such a way that we live what God wills. This doesn't happen by trying to be like the world.

All through Israel's history, they battled against the temptation to join the world around them and follow its ways. They kept leaving God, committing adultery with the world, and suffering the devastating consequences.

Why is it so hard for us to learn from the Israelites the devastation of "loving the world"? (1 John 2:13-17; 5:19). Why can we not just accept that we are different, in fact, that we are called to be different? (Remember, that is what holy means—to be separate, distinct or other, to be different as God is.)

The modern teaching of becoming more like the world in order to win the world is like a giant whirlpool that sucks us in. It is a false teaching. Why so? Because we can never be enough like the world until we are right in the center of it, and then it is too late!

Many from Anabaptist groups are trying to blend in with the world around them. On Sunday we sing: *"Spirit of God, descend upon my heart / Wean it from earth; through all its pulses move…,"* but on Monday we rush to the secondhand store to get good deals on clothes that make us look like everybody else—and that isn't turning out right. Slowly, ever-changing fashions replace simplicity and humility. As a result we lose our freedom and come under the ruling power and discipleship of this world's fashions. We select skirts and blouses, extra ruffles and adornments, and more casual head coverings in an attempt to narrow the gap and fit in to the surrounding society. In the Mennonite areas of

Pennsylvania, Ohio, and Manitoba, these changes simply identify one as a more liberal Mennonite (and there are many of them
around). But take that same more liberal person who blended into
Lancaster county, Pennsylvania and move them to Quebec City in
Canada and they will suddenly stand out as an ultra-conservative.
So then what? What accommodations and compromises will they
have to make to *feel* not too different in Quebec?

It is time to wake up and realize that we and multitudes of other
churches have believed a lie. The evangelical denomination to which
I belonged in the 1980s had an underlying concern that we were too
different from the world. The more conservative and modest styles
of dress slowly changed to conform to the fashions of the surrounding world. The contemporary Christian music tried to imitate the
music of the day as closely as allowable. Certain doctrines and practices that would be offensive to the world slowly disappeared, but
none of that was enough. We still saw ourselves as too different! So
what next?

In the years since, many evangelical churches, in their desire to
grow, have stopped talking about sin, or about the blood of Jesus,
or about repentance—and instead serve coffee and doughnuts and
give dance lessons. They call it being seeker sensitive. The Bible calls
it being like the world. So, brothers and sisters, at what point will you
be enough like the world? Beware! Do not be fooled by the world. It
is a deceptive whirlpool.

Jesus Himself said that few would follow Him. Like Him, we are not
here to condemn the world but to point those who will follow to the
right way. Paul exhorts us, "Come out from among them [the world],
and be ye separate [remember, that means holy]… and [then] ye
shall be my sons and daughters…" (2 Corinthians 6:14-18) He says
there can be no fellowship with unrighteousness and no communion
with darkness. Jesus said to His unconverted brothers, "*The world
cannot hate you* [because you still belong to it]; but **me it hateth**,
[why?] because I testify of it [the world], that the works thereof are

evil" (John 7:7, emphasis added). Months later, He made a totally different statement about His own disciples: "I have given them thy word; and **the world hath hated them**, [why?] because *they are not of the world*, even as I am not of the world" (John 17:14, 16, emphasis added). His brothers were not hated because they belonged to the world. But His disciples were hated because they belonged to Christ and were shaped by His Word.

Let me ask you, can you trust the world? Should you blend in with it? Can you, as a Christian, follow its lifestyle, values, fashions, entertainment, and materialism? No, rather you must distrust it. You must hold it suspect. You must recognize it as enemy territory and even enemy culture!

3. Thirdly, then, we must recognize that God's people are *a minority, prophetic people.* They are to be an alternative society, a replacement society, one that demonstrates another option, another lifestyle— that of the kingdom of heaven.

   Prophets are not always popular. They point out where the church and the world are going wrong. They also call it back to what God originally intended. The church, as God's called-out people, is to be a prophetic model and pattern for others to observe and to choose to follow. We are not called to be just a little bit better than those around us.

   We are called to set a whole new direction that takes its starting point from the Bible revelation of God's will, and *not* from the way things are done in the society around us. We are to be salt in society, to be like a little leaven (yeast) in bread and like light in the dark. This is a high, holy, and important calling. Will we heed it or trade it for something easier (like being a U-boat in a museum)? Minorities who live God's way can make an impact. At least they did in the first three hundred years of the church.

4. Remember, we stated earlier that *there are two distinctly different understandings of the church:*

- A separate, prophetic new society and new culture that *replaces* the society and culture of the world

—*or*—

- A collection of individuals gathered to hear sermons, sing, and evangelize, but retain active membership in the society and popular culture that surrounds them

We could illustrate this difference with two diagrams:

For the first diagram, imagine just one big circle. It represents the society around about us. In the middle of this society is the church building with its people, pews, and programs. In that building, Christian hockey players, race car drivers, Kung Fu experts, dancers, models, politicians, soldiers, and money lovers gather to learn to pray, but they never have to leave their world-shaped culture and society. They can learn to pray, but share values, occupations, and goals that Jesus Christ would never share.

The second diagram has not one circle, but two. The first is the surrounding society with its values, practices, and priorities and the thousands of ways in which these things are fleshed out and applied in their culture. Beside this is another circle. It is the new society of God's people with their values and purposes and thus, thousands of practical expressions of a new culture that is shaped by the pillars of kingdom Christianity. They have left their former circle and the dominating influence of one society (this present evil world), and have exchanged it for another. Citizenship in this new world calls for renewed thinking in order to restore what God originally intended.

A great gap exists between these two types of churches. They are very different in their nature and their purpose, and yet amazingly, many people from Anabaptist backgrounds want to find a church somewhere between these two types. They want a church that is still *somewhat* conservative, but not as distinct from the rest of society. They want liberty to be given to individuals to apply Scripture apart from the church. These seekers of a somewhere-in-between-church have failed to see the two distinct and even opposite concepts of the church. They simply have a *personal preference* for a slightly more conservative setting, just as some people prefer a more teaching-oriented church or a charismatic one.

Some details of church life are not spelled out in the Bible. There is room for variety. But we would do well to study and build on what the Bible does say—that the church is to be a separated, prophetic people. If our choice of church leads us away from this emphasis, then we are departing from the church of the Bible and replacing it with one that suits our personal taste.

> ### *Blessings*
> #### *of Embracing Pillar 3:*
>
> *Benefits of peoplehood:*
>
> - *God is at work creating a people for His own possession.*
> - *He has called this people to be a new society that restores and lives all that He originally intended.*
> - *I can be part of this community of faith, hope, and joy.*
> - *God fills my heart with love for my brothers.*
> - *My brothers' burdens become my concern.*
> - *When struggles come, we confess and pray together.*
> - *When disaster strikes, others are there to help.*
> - *We give ourselves to "the apostles' teaching, to fellowship, the breaking of bread and prayer."*
> - *We have a "koinonia" society.*

5. A society or nation is *bigger* than an independent individual, *bigger* than independent ministers and missionaries, and also *bigger* than just one local church. The American spirit of independence and the fear of having anyone tell us what to do have greatly influenced much of the church and her ministers. It has kept us from the united witness and vitality of the book of Acts. It has left us as small, isolated, local churches, struggling alone to survive in an increasingly hostile and self-centered culture.

If the great design of all history is God's desire for a distinct and holy people who manifest His oneness, wisdom and glory, then we would be greatly blessed if we as individuals, ministers, and local churches could break the stronghold of independence and in humility build a strong, new society that stands together, proclaiming and modeling the lifestyle of God's kingdom.

6. If the understanding presented here of the church as a distinct and separate replacement society is biblical, then *we must teach it more clearly* to our people as a key part of the foundation or skeleton upon which we make practical applications. If we fail to understand the foundational nature, joy, and calling of this new society we simply will be burdened with a set of rules that often are not understood.

    Furthermore, if this new society is the finished product and goal that God has always had in mind, then our primary function as ministers, bishops, and brotherhoods must also be to embrace this ultimate purpose and to ensure that our preaching, meetings, decisions, and plans lead the whole church towards its fulfillment.

7. To be a people, *we must be intentionally involved in daily areas of each other's lives,* and not just in weekly worship or occasional fellowship and activities. In too much of modern church life we are disconnected from one another vocationally, geographically, socially, and economically. This is not a new society. The reality of becoming such a society will not just happen. It will take much study, prayer, planning, and probably openness to the counsel and fellowship of those who are further ahead on that road.

8. This new, holy, prophetic people *was birthed by the Holy Spirit* at Pentecost. It was the remarkable work of the Spirit that marked the whole book of Acts. It was the Spirit that moved in the upper room. It was the Spirit that was poured out on three thousand. The Spirit united hearts and moved men to share all they had. Without this visible outpouring of the Holy Spirit, there would have been no new people, no holy standard, no bold missions, and, in short, no difference from the Old Testament experience. The book of Acts is not the record of a social revolution or of a doctrinal reform. It is not the record of men with a new understanding of their duty to God or a

new resolve to obey Him. No, it is about a whole new thing, about the Spirit moving on men and women, ushering them into a spiritual reality they had never known before.

It can be no different today. If we as God's people are not first a community clearly endued with the Spirit, then how is it that we can call ourselves God's people? God's longing and design is still for a holy people, and the only way to birth and sustain such a community is still the same. It is the result of the work and power of the Holy Spirit.

If you still aren't convinced that God's design is for us somehow to be His people, read what it says will be the reality in the new heavens and new earth: "Behold, the tabernacle of God is with man, and He will dwell with them, and they shall be His **people**, and God Himself shall be with them, and be their God (Revelation 21:1-3, emphasis added).

MEMORY AID

- Pillar 1—COMMUNION—**God exists**—He is central, and our relationship to Him gives meaning to all of life.

- Pillar 2—COMMUNICATION—**God has spoken**—I can know and do His will.

- Pillar 3—COMMUNITY—**Peoplehood**—God's central design and purpose is to have a distinct people who are like Him.

- Pillar 4—CITIZENSHIP—**The Kingdom of God**—This next pillar is critical for guiding our lives as His new people.

Seeds of the Faith—Pillar 4

The faith stands as mighty pillars, solid and unchanging. It rises as glorious mountain peaks, but it began its work in me as little seeds.

Bible study, body ministry, community—these are wonderful parts of the Christian life—but as I read my Bible what kept jumping off the page was that God is holy. He didn't just want a nice community; He wanted a holy, separated people. But what does that mean? What does a holy people look like?

As I look back thirty-five years, I realize that multitudes of Christians who were introduced to the Spirit-filled life and body ministry never grasped the holiness of God. They never became a holy people, and today I don't want to be where many of them are.

So, what was missing?

It might be an oversimplification, but it seems that before my time, two generations of evangelicals had been raised in dispensationalist churches—raised with much talk of the rapture and the end times and little thought about the life God expected now. In fact, the teaching was that God's kingdom had been delayed. It was for later, not for now. My peers at Bible school were weary of the pessimistic end times focus and attracted by the new church growth movement and by the huge megachurches that were popping up. But me? I found a book on New Testament theology that spoke of the kingdom of God not as a future reality, but as now. I went to my Bible, and there it was over and over—the kingdom has come. Kingdom living is for now. I somehow knew that this was a key to understanding the New Testament and the plan of God, but it was twenty more years before I realized how big this discovery really was.

PILLAR 4

The Kingdom of God

We believe that God's heavenly kingdom has been brought to earth—now—by His Son Jesus. We, as a Christian people, are the citizens and subjects of that kingdom, and not of the political and economic kingdoms of this world.

Two Kingdoms

I live close to the border of Canada and the United States. We cross that border fairly often, but we are always aware of that line. Do we have our passports? Will they let us through? Will we get interrogated? You see, the border is a real geographic boundary that I can see and cross.

The kingdom of God is also a very real, very visible, and very different government, but there is no border station on earth at which I pass into it. I have no passport book stamped by the King, and yet the kingdom of God existed before the earth was here and will be there when Canada and the United States are no more. It is bigger than any geography and goes beyond history. Its King actually owns all lands, and His subjects, or people, are found all over the globe.

Traveling as a family in the United States, we have often exclaimed, "This looks so American!" It was obvious that we were not in Canada.

It was so obvious to us that even if we had been sleeping in the back-seat when we went through the border, we could have awakened in some small town and known we were in the United States. The houses and fences are different. The stores, banks, and churches all look different.

That same obvious difference is to be seen clearly in the values and whole manner of life of God's kingdom people. God's people are called to make the kingdom of heaven visible wherever they are! There is to be a clear distinction between the citizens of this world's kingdom and the people of God's kingdom.

Ultimately, only two kingdoms exist on earth, and they are in deadly conflict and opposition to each other: (1) the kingdom of this world, and (2) the kingdom of Heaven (or the kingdom of God).

The Bible says that we as God's people and His subjects:

- Have been delivered from Kingdom 1, this present evil world, or age (Galatians 1:4).

- Are now to "live...soberly, righteously, and godly [where?] in this present world" as a "peculiar people," purified unto God (Titus 2:12-14).

- Have been delivered from the power (ruling influence) of darkness of the present world and have been "translated into [Kingdom 2], the kingdom of his dear Son" (Colossians 1:13). That word *translated* means to be moved from one distinct place to another distinct place. In other words, a border is crossed. One moves from being a citizen in the world to being a citizen of heaven; someone who lives in enemy territory here in the world.

Jesus Himself told the Jews,

> "*Ye are from beneath;*
> *I am from above:*
> *Ye are of this world;*
> *I am not of this world*" (John 8:23).

John, the beloved apostle, stated:

"We know that we [believers] are of God."

—and, on the other hand,—

"The whole world lieth in wickedness" (1 John 5:19).

No Dual Citizens

These are serious and very strong statements indicating that there are two distinct realities or countries and that we cannot be dual citizens. We belong to one or the other. The world has rejected our King, rejected His lordship over all of life, and rejected His new society, laws, directions, and values. In other words, the world is the enemy of Christ and of the believer.

When Jesus came to earth, it was with a mission. That mission was not to come and start a new reformed synagogue or new services once a week as a compartment of our lives. No, He came to dethrone the enemy. He came to bring in and reestablish in seed form, the kingdom of God— that is, the government and life of heaven.

John the Baptist, Jesus, and Paul all came preaching the arrival of this new government and kingdom of God on earth (e.g. Matthew 3:2;

> ## *Consequences*
> ### *of Ignoring Pillar 4:*
>
> *Results of dual citizenship:*
>
> - *Mixing with the world is the sin of Balaam. By doing so, we destroy God's society.*
>
> - *We belong to the same kingdom as everyone else.*
>
> - *There is no clear separation between us and the kingdom of this world.*
>
> - *We are confused because we are trying to keep both worlds happy.*
>
> - *We uncritically accept much of the values, priorities, and mindset of this present evil world.*
>
> - *We are lured by the world's advertising to covet the things that it offers.*
>
> - *Our styles and fashions keep changing because the world's spirit of fashion is in our hearts.*
>
> - *We get involved in warfare, competition, and politics, thus compromising our position and testimony in God's kingdom.*
>
> - *We seek the world's approval, and want those we are trying to reach to accept us.*

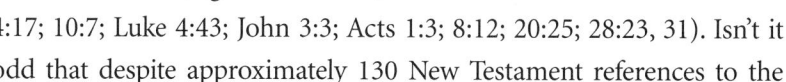

4:17; 10:7; Luke 4:43; John 3:3; Acts 1:3; 8:12; 20:25; 28:23, 31). Isn't it odd that despite approximately 130 New Testament references to the kingdom of God, a host of evangelical preachers and scholars have relegated the kingdom and the values it promotes to a future age after the tribulation? Isn't it disturbing to consider that Paul preached the Lord Jesus and His kingdom right to his final days, but most today preach a Jesus without His kingdom and without His radical teaching? The glorious peaks of the kingdom have all too often been hidden behind the clouds of human reasoning that rob the believer of a full picture of the Gospel. It is our job as kingdom Christians to change this and to see that the central theme of the Gospel is preached in the entire world.

Practically, what does that mean? What actually needs to be preached? What are they not hearing? The people of the kingdom are seeking to discern, model, and proclaim the life, relationships, purposes, and values that God intended from the beginning. Relevant kingdom preaching tackles the needs of the day and applies the words and character of Christ to those needs. It talks about anger, lust, purity in courtship, money, greed, idolatry, hate, war, headship order, the role of males and females, parenting, divorce and remarriage, music, media and, in short, all the areas that make up our lives. Kingdom preaching does not excuse our failures in these areas, but calls God's Spirit-filled community to discover and fulfill the righteous plan of God.

Now remember, this kingdom we are to proclaim is very different from the power structures of this world. This kingdom of Jesus was not brought in by revolution or war, by politics or power. It did not change the world by using the wealth of the rich, by promoting education, or by encouraging Christians to become doctors, lawyers, and judges. No, Jesus said if His kingdom were of this world, He would have used their worldly methods, but it is not of this world. Rather, His revolution began at the bottom with the poor, the uneducated, and the needy. It began with giving instead of grasping, with kindness instead of cursing, with laying down our lives for others, with humility and gentleness. It began when men, instead of seeking material gain, power, and position, began to "seek first the kingdom of God" (Matthew 6:33, 34).

Please note that when I settle which kingdom I choose to join, it simplifies all of life. It simplifies my choices, because it removes the worry of trying to fit into the changing culture of the day. It frees me from being self-conscious about what my neighbors think of me. I expect their disapproval, for they are citizens of the other kingdom. "Marvel not, my brethren, if the world hate you" (1 John 3:13).

I think that it bears repeating here that you and I must not be like the world to win it. This is the opposite of the kingdom message, which says we are salt and light in the world. Salt has no real value until it is put on the meat. A flashlight is most useful when it is turned on in the dark, not in the daylight. The salt and the light are valuable because they are so different from the meat and darkness. We too, are different, and it is only because we are different that we can offer any lasting help and hope to the people around us.

Ten Years Behind the World?

By now it should be apparent that it is in these two points:

Being a distinct people (Pillar 3),

—and —

Being under the government or kingdom of God right now (Pillar 4),

that the Radical Believers' Churches foundationally differ from much of the Christendom of today. The modern church accepts that we are dual citizens, married to Christ and to our country. They say we are to be involved in politics, in warfare, in society, and in the culture that surrounds us. We belong to the world as worldlings, but with slightly higher values.

By this way of reckoning, where the world is today the church will be in ten years (or maybe two). In other words, the modern church is slightly more conservative than the world but is going the same direction, just a little more slowly. This is not what Jesus came to initiate. He came to lay a different foundation for life and to set an opposing direction.

The Kingdom Laws—Did Jesus Mean What He Said?

The Radical Believers' Churches recognize that the teachings and commandments of Jesus are the laws of the kingdom for the church today. They especially turn to the serious statements of Christ in the Sermon on the Mount (Matthew 5-7; Luke 6:17-49).

On the other hand, many evangelical churches downplay the teachings of the Sermon on the Mount and Hebrews or make them something for a future millennial age. The hard sayings of Jesus are made easier, so that lust, anger, materialism, covetousness, and divorce are somehow not as serious as what Jesus said. Jesus is now a nice guy whose main message is that we must just love and accept everybody and not judge.

But this is not the Jesus who upset the Jews and Romans, and was crucified on a cross. It is not the message that turned the Roman Empire upside down in three hundred years. It is not the message that has caused multitudes to suffer persecution and loss of life and family.

The modern Jesus and the popular gospel of America make the church "right side up" again—just like the world. It makes the church and the world friends (James 4:4), and has robbed the Gospel and Christian life of its power.

We must get back to the Gospel of the real King Jesus and His kingdom. All through history, little groups have separated from the masses of Christendom to seek to reinstate a vision for an obedient kingdom people. They usually have been ridiculed, persecuted, and called legalists by the world churches of their day. So this fourth pillar of the literal kingdom of God breaking into the present evil world is a critically important and foundational pillar of what true churches throughout history have believed.

Let me share how suddenly seeing this pillar of the kingdom changed my life and the direction of my family.

I had first preached the Sermon on the Mount and the kingdom of God as an eleven-year-old boy in our home in Zambia. Later, in Bible school, I again saw the centrality of this message in the New Testament, and it became a prominent theme of my preaching and direction over the next eleven years. But somehow what I believed and taught was robbed of its power because I, like everyone else I knew, saw myself as a dual citizen. I was under the government of God and of this world. I was to obey God and be an acceptable part of the culture of this world. I was to be a responsible citizen doing my part by voting and lobbying for political change. I was to preach the kingdom and yet be like the world to win it.

Eventually these two kingdoms collided. A Reformed Baptist pastor introduced us to a doctrine that, if adopted and practiced would set us very definitely at odds with our Canadian society. What were we to do? The teaching introduced was the doctrine of the headship covering or veiling for women. After much study, my wife and I acknowledged that what the Scripture said seemed to be indisputable, but there were always reasons not to obey—primarily two. First, we

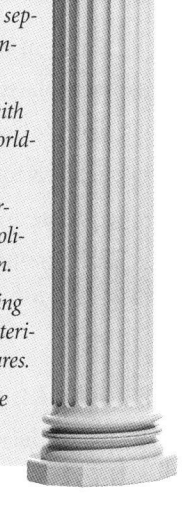

Blessings
of Embracing Pillar 4:

Benefits of a two-kingdom faith:

- *We are citizens in an alternative kingdom. Knowing this brings clarity and freedom to life.*

- *We are unapologetically separated from and non-conformed to this world.*

- *We are being renewed with a kingdom mind and worldview.*

- *We are free from the warfare, competition, and politics of this world's system.*

- *We are free from the ruling influence of fashion, materialism, and fleshly pleasures.*

- *We expect and accept the rejection of this world.*

stumbled over seeming inconsistencies in the lives of people who practiced covering the head. Second, we were concerned about how we could reach others if we looked so different.

Some time later I listened to a series of tapes on nonconformity and nonresistance in every area of life. My eyes were opened, and I saw that I had been holding to two opposing doctrines—one I openly preached, God's kingdom, and other a doctrine I never preached, "being like the world to win the world." If you had asked me whether I believed in that latter doctrine I would have vigorously denied it, and yet it affected all I did.

Once I fully accepted that I was a citizen of God's kingdom and no other, and that I was a part of His distinct and separate people and of no other, then several areas of disobedience evaporated. I no longer had to balance obedience to God with concern over what my neighbor would think. Our reasons to resist the head covering disappeared. They were just cultural reasons that had kept us from obedience. Our desire to not look too different from the world changed and we took more steps towards dressing modestly and not following the fashions, fads, jewels, and materialism of the world around us. Our views on involvement in politics, war, rights, insurance, media, competition, and culture all were affected.

It is important for you to note that all these changes we made were not just isolated pet issues. No, they all were connected to and sprang out of our foundational understanding that we were now unapologetically a part of another kingdom. So with that new understanding, I first sought to please and obey my King and what He has commanded, and only then did I go out to win the world.

Critical Pillars

Three times in the preceding paragraphs I have stated that much of the modern Protestant church has been robbed of this full understanding of the two opposing kingdoms and of the practical applications of that doctrine. I am not saying that someone has purposefully altered the Gospel. In fact, most of them don't know anything is missing. Rather, I am pulling back the clouds for you. If a Realtor sold you a house but never told you that behind the nicely-veneered basement walls was a crumbling foundation, you would not be very happy. Let's put it another way. If he did his job and informed you that the house you wanted to buy had a bad foundation, would you be angry with him? You might be because he spoiled your dream, but I hope you would thank him.

If you choose to accept my report of God's distinct, present kingdom rule, then some of your worldly dreams and ideas will be spoiled, and instead of the broad religious road of easier, cost-free Christianity, you will find yourself on the narrow and costly road that Jesus described.

I have introduced to you some critical information about kingdom foundations. It is for you to determine what you will do with this information. Your choices will impact your future one way or the other, but don't be afraid. You just need to start where you are and begin, by faith, to take little steps of obedience. I have tried to help you see how serious this pillar is, but please, I hope you don't think it is too hard and ugly. Quite the contrary, good foundations, healthy skeletons, and clear mountain vistas contribute to the beauty of life, and so it is with the treasures of kingdom Christianity.

MEMORY AID

- Pillar 1—COMMUNION—**God exists**—He is not just all powerful, but also His very nature is relational.

- Pillar 2—COMMUNICATION—**God has spoken**—I can hear what He has to say, so I am without excuse.

- Pillar 3—COMMUNITY—**Peoplehood**—God has called us to be a whole new race or people-group that models the love, unity, and relationships of the Trinity.

- Pillar 4—CITIZENSHIP—**The Kingdom of God**—Our citizenship has been transferred to a kingdom that in the opinion of the world is all upside down and backward.

- Pillar 5—COMMITMENT—**Discipleship**—Being part of God's kingdom people is a serious and costly business.

Seeds of the Faith—Pillar 5

The faith stands as mighty pillars, solid and unchanging. It rises as glorious mountain peaks, but it began its work in me as little seeds.

My bookshelf is full of titles such as Discipleship, Multiplying Disciples, *and* The Lost Art of Disciple Making. *Perhaps the "lost art" says it best. As I look back over my years as a Christian, I wonder, did anyone purposefully disciple me? Did anyone have a long-term goal in mind and think, "This is the kind of person I want to help David become"?*

I wish I could say a seed of the importance of discipleship was planted in me because someone first purposefully invested in my life.

As I began seriously studying my Bible, it became very clear that Jesus called men to be with Him to be taught by Him and to be sent out in His name. This whole process was called making disciples. As a soon-to-be minister, I didn't want to merely preach sermons. I wanted to make disciples. There was a seed planted in me, and it went deep, but I also felt a sense of agony, of lostness. How can I do this? I sensed, even then, that discipleship is more than just a program. Jesus called men to be with Him. He spent his life with them. They became a discipling community. I didn't have that, so how could I do what He did? It became apparent that there were two lost arts: discipleship and actual communities committed to that disciple-making process. I longed for both but had no idea how to get there. A seed was planted, however, and somehow I knew that God desired communities that were committed to discipleship.

That disciple-making community seems a long way off, but the seed has been planted, and I'm still on my way there.

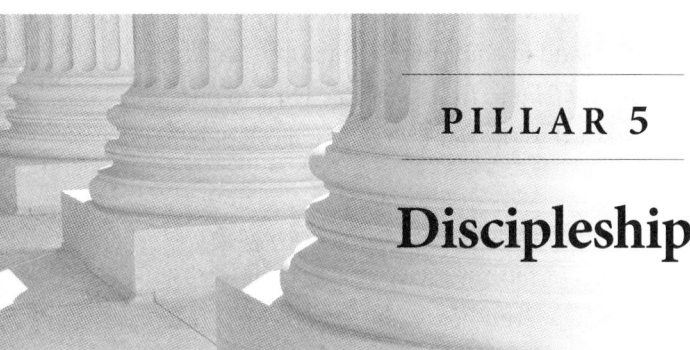

PILLAR 5

Discipleship

We believe that we are called to be disciples of Jesus, following Him in all of life, and that we are called to make disciples of others.

Be Disciples and Make Disciples

Did a godly believer ever say to you, "Come and follow me, watch me and do as I do?" Have you ever invited others to follow you and do as you do?

Likely your answer to both of these questions is no. In our individualistic world, it just seems too arrogant and bossy to actually request such things of others. Many even hesitate to give their own children and young people this kind of direction. But calling others to follow is what Jesus did, what Paul did, and what Jewish rabbis before them had done. It is called being a disciple and making disciples.

Discipleship has two significant parts:

1. Disciples (learners) are *called to follow*—Jesus is their Pattern.

    The two previous pillars clearly showed God has a people (Pillar 3) and a kingdom (Pillar 4). Pillar 5 confronts us with God's call to discipleship. He personally calls men and women to leave all—to forsake their priorities, reputation, success, ideas, independence and wealth—and to come and be a part of that kingdom people, *to come and follow* Him, to imitate Him, to pursue Him and press on upward to the mark of the high call of being like Him.

The kingdom is not a vague, undefined reality. No, *Jesus Himself* says to come and "Learn of me, for my yoke is easy [it works, it fits] and my burden is light [not heavy and impossible]" (Matthew 11:28-30). He will teach us. He has specific ways for us to follow. He is a *King* who governs with very definite and good laws that make all of life work and bring us into a place of rest. He also is a *Teacher* who knows how to step by step bring us into that obedience and rest (Matthew 11:28; Exodus 33:14; Jeremiah 6:16).

The disciple is one who answers this call to come and be with Jesus—to be in the presence of Jesus. He comes to learn the teachings of Jesus and the end goal is that he, the disciple, will be able to live out those teachings in real life and become like his Teacher (Luke 6:40; Matthew 10:25).

> *The Teacher is holding up a pattern for the disciple to follow, and the disciple is submitting to the pattern.*

2. Disciples are *called to make more followers*—to teach and to be a pattern for others!

Being a follower is one side of what discipleship means. The second significant thing about the pillar of discipleship is that we as believers and churches are called to make disciples of others. That truly is an incredible thing that *we*, on behalf of our Teacher, are to call others to come!

> *We are to teach, to model His life, and to be a pattern for others to follow.*

Let me emphasize that this call to make disciples is not just a course, not simply going through a book of beliefs or a catechism. It is much more. Jesus did not just take the masses through a study book. Nor can we. He had a few men who shared life with Him. They were involved in all of life together. They were a community, a people; teaching was in life, not just in a classroom. So it must be with us.

To disciple others is practical. It is the "how to" of kingdom living. Jesus' last command (and last words are important) was "Go ye, therefore [literally, this reads "going therefore" or "as ye go"] and teach [make disciples of] all nations." And what are we to teach? "Teach them *to observe* [to obey] *all things* whatsoever I have commanded you" (Matthew 28:19-20).

Paul later charged Timothy, his disciple, in a similar way: "The things that thou hast heard of me among many witnesses, the same commit [deposit] thou to faithful men, who shall be able to teach others also" (2 Timothy 2:2).

Paul says to the Thessalonian church: "And ye became followers [literally mimics or imitators] of us, and of the Lord, having received the word in much affliction, with the joy of the Holy Ghost; so that [in turn] ye were ensamples [that is, types or patterns to follow] to

Consequences
of Ignoring Pillar 5:

Results of not actively engaging in discipleship:

- *Each individual becomes his own authority. He sets his own values and convictions. He disciples himself.*

- *Our teaching and discipling cannot be done with authority because everyone practices something different.*

- *There is confusion because of disunity.*

- *Our convictions are weakened because they are not acted on.*

- *Our young men hear inspiring teaching on their responsibility, decision making, and leadership, but seeing no example in the older men, they soon turn to materialism, toys, and selfish pursuits.*

- *Our young sisters get a vision of godly womanhood, but they see few examples and get little affirmation from the church. Soon their conviction in this and many other areas weakens and begins to disappear.*

- *The message comes across that we don't really mean what we preach.*

- *When we finally wake up to our failure, the mess is so big that we don't know what to do.*

all that believe in Macedonia and Achaia" (1 Thessalonians 1:6-7). In 1 Thessalonians 2:13-14, Paul says they "received the word of God . . . not as the word of men, but as it is in truth, the word of God ... which works in you... For ye brethren, became followers [this is that word imitators again] of the churches of God ... in Judaea."

There it is. Paul is a model or pattern for Timothy and for the Thessalonians. They have the same pattern in the churches of Judea, and they at Thessalonica in turn became a pattern of godly life for the new believers in Macedonia and Achaia. This is no ugly authoritarianism. It is an invitation to a life that works and displays its beauty and harmony for all to see.

I have worked in three different truss shops in my life. It is very important when you assemble trusses (roof rafters) that all the pieces get cut precisely according to a pattern. If they are not, the roof line will be very crooked. Likewise, a mother gives her daughter a pattern for a dress to sew, or a recipe for making pecan pie, and she expects her daughter to stick to the pattern. Why? Because it works. In the same way, Paul calls us as communities to multiply and pass on a pattern of a godly style of life that creates a straight and beautiful roof line on the building of God.

Not Orphans, But Disciples

It is popular today both on the mission field and at home, to say, *"Just bring people to Jesus and let Jesus teach them how to live."* This sounds spiritual, but it is not. It neatly sets aside the command to make disciples and the command for those new disciples to submit to a new pattern of life and the culture of a whole new godly society passed down to them.

A group of Anabaptist ministers shared that their greatest discouragement was to preach and give direction, only to be ignored by the congregation. A minister's wife seeks to give counsel in a sisters' meeting and the report is she is too legalistic. One church member feels computers are of the anti-Christ, another advocates accountability and screening, and still another thinks we need to trust God to protect us as we use the Internet. All of these are "spiritual" people. What do we do? The crux of the matter is that if we do not have an agreement about what we teach and practice it will be just each person doing and believing what they *feel* is right.

If the local church is composed of individuals who all believe and do what they think is right, then there is little point having elders, there is no room for authoritative preaching, and church becomes just a place you go to hear a nice speech and socialize.

The Christian life is not just me and my God. I have been joined to a people, a family that has a specific set of governing values. Just as a child is taught the ways of his or her family, or an Eskimo is taught the laws of his or her culture, so the new believer is discipled and shown the pattern of life in the kingdom of God (1 Corinthians 4:16-17; 11:1-2, 16; 7:17; 14:33; 2 Thessalonians 3:7, 9; Titus 2:7; Philippians 3:17; Hebrews 6:12; 13:7).

The Faith Is Ethical—It Teaches Us How to Live

You see, a distinctive mark of the Radical Believers' Church is her confession that the faith is ethical. It has to do with behavior. It has to do with how I am to live. The discipling church takes its faith in the revealed Word of God and applies it to the needs and issues of the day.

A powerful example of this is found in the book of Titus. In Titus 2:11-12, we read that "the grace of God that bringeth salvation has appeared to all men [and what does it do?] *teaching* us that denying ungodliness and worldly lusts, we should live soberly, righteously, and godly in this present world."

These two verses tell us that God has provided something called grace that comes into our lives as a life-giving teacher. This teacher helps us identify and deal with evil, with bad fruit, with grey areas, and with questionable and confusing practices. It helps us make godly, fruit-bearing choices about practical things we face in the world around us such as books, movies, Internet, video games, social networking, television, dancing, alcohol, drugs, gambling, pornography. God's grace, coming as a wonderful teacher, calls me to deny and break with worldly lusts and to actually live a sober and righteous life.

Where true grace and salvation are at work, worldly lusts and idols will be toppled. Empire building, fame, position, riches, pleasure, the idolatry of sports—all these areas will come under the guidance of practical discipleship.

If we look at the entire second chapter of Titus, it is not just every man figuring out for himself what is right in these areas. Rather, the church is also seeking God and applying the Word together to the situations and dangers of the day, corporately modeling a pattern of godliness. She is discussing and teaching what soberness is. Old men, filled with grace, are teaching young men to identify foolish pursuits and behavior and to avoid them. They are teaching them to be faithful workers, to submit to authority. They teach godly, hands-off courtship and purity instead of the promiscuous dating spirit of our age. They teach the permanence of marriage as Jesus declared it. They teach financial faithfulness and the importance of sound and edifying speech.

The older women, filled with God's grace, teach the younger how to act in a pure, quiet, and holy way, how to be discreet and modest, and how to handle their emotions. They teach them practical ways to be keepers at home and how actually to love their husbands. They teach headship order and submission. In Titus 2 these practical teachings are called "sound doctrine" (verses 1, 10) and "a pattern of good works" (verse 7). God's grace comes as a teacher and that same grace actively works in God's people so that we too can teach.

Can you see it? Discipleship happens not in a classroom, but in the community. Someone is teaching you. Some community is shaping how you live as a people. The great question is, who are your teachers? Jesus has given this job of practical teaching in all of life to the church. Remember His last words, "Go therefore into all nations and make disciples . . . teaching them to obey all the things I have commanded you."

Not a Creed to Believe, but a Godly Life in Christ

Unfortunately, discipleship is most often wrongly thought to be explaining what we believe about God, salvation, the Trinity, and other doctrines, so in the end, we could pass a test and know the right answers.

In contrast to this, we believe *the focus of discipleship is instruction in how to live godly in Christ Jesus.* It is providing both teaching and a model for others to follow soberly in life.

A discipling church knows what it believes as facts, but it also knows how to live as the new distinctive society and culture of God's people. Thus *its members are able, with one mind, to teach, preach, disciple, correct, and, discipline as needed.* A group of individuals or families teaching or doing what is right in their own eyes could never produce this united witness of a new community seen in Scripture. A parent disciples and trains up a child in the way he should go so that when he is mature he will not depart from it. Likewise, a church trains up, models, and calls believers to follow in the way of the new people of God. Just as Chinese teach children to be Chinese by instruction and example, so the church disciples people to be truly Christian.

The Chinese are not Chinese because they know China's history and beliefs, for even you and I can do that. It takes more than that to be Chinese and more than that to be a Christian disciple.

Most churches know their history and the doctrine or facts they believe and around which they have unity. They know what facts they believe differently from the facts believed by another church group. Yet the lives and behavior of both church groups often are very similar to each other, and unfortunately, also very similar to the world!

The point then of being a discipling people is that we instruct in

1. The facts

   —and—

2. The practice—that is, in how we should now live distinct from the world and clearly separated unto God

Both of these together make up what Paul calls sound doctrine (sound teaching). If we, in our instruction and example, are missing the second point, then we are not purposefully making disciples, and we miss a large part of our calling.

My Discipleship Puzzle

One thing that puzzled me when I first came into contact with Anabaptist people and their writings was their use of the word *discipleship*. They talked much of discipleship and even claimed that one big difference between themselves and the Protestant evangelical churches was their emphasis on discipleship.

Coming from my Protestant background, I reached the opposite conclusion. It seemed the Anabaptists had no time to disciple because they were so busy working to make a living. And if they did have time, they had no actual program to do so, except maybe a pre-baptism class.

The Protestants, on the other hand, had whole libraries of books describing one-on-one discipling, group discipling, multiplying disciples, and sharing the faith. They had an incredible stock of resources that could be used to give direction and guidance to the disciple. So what was the difference? Who really emphasized discipleship? I think the answer is both. Eventually, I came to learn that for the Anabaptist, *discipleship meant obedience in all of life*. Without growth in obedience to the teachings of Christ, they believed there was no discipleship. They rightly saw that discipleship involved all of life and not just class time.

The problem, however, is that there are still men and women, young and old, who need to be systematically taught the basics of the Christian faith, practice, and witness. All too often we Anabaptists have no sound resources to do so, and no people who have been trained to take on this joyful task. Here the Protestants can teach us, for they have men freed up to develop resources, to train laborers, and to do the actual work of discipling.

To my dying day, I'm sure I will remember the different men who after experiencing great revival in their lives and joining the church, shared their desire and even expectation that they would be meeting with me at least once a week. Oh, the agony to know I could not meet their expectation and that there was no one else prepared to do so.

Our own church's birth was the result of a great move of God. Its great failure was its lack of preparation to make disciples of those who came. If we are to make disciples, we must know what we are aiming for, how we are going to get there, and who is going to do the job. We must not just talk of discipleship. We must train and free men up to do it. We desperately need both the Anabaptist and Protestant understandings of discipleship.

Even as I am revising this book, I am using these basic pillars and Scriptures as an outline for discipling another brother, and what a delight it is for both of us! But brethren, if sickness, church struggles and a period of semi-retirement from fulltime work had not freed me up, I would never have started this book, nor used it as a tool to disciple my brother.

What must we do to take the King's call to make disciples seriously? What will He have to do to us if we will not change our ways and give heed to this vital command?

I know one dear brother with a gift of discipleship who was freed up and sent out to use his gift. As a result, four or five churches were helped and established on a good foundation. May his tribe and the tribe of those who sent him increase. There can indeed be many more men like this dear servant if we will just give ourselves to preparing disciples and then sending out disciple-makers to do what he has done.

Blessings
of Embracing Pillar 5:

Benefits of the disciple-making community:

- *Discipleship happens in the community of faith.*

- *Our values and convictions are shared and built together.*

- *We can teach and model a common, agreed-upon doctrine and practice.*

- *Our values and convictions are strengthened because we together act on what we teach and experience the blessings of that obedience.*

- *Our young men learn responsibility, decision making, and leadership by being with men who have these qualities.*

- *Our young ladies learn a quiet spirit by being taught, encouraged, and corrected by a community of quiet, submissive sisters.*

- *The message comes across that we live what we preach.*

- *The church grows in conviction and joy as it is built up in the faith.*

The Cost and Conditions of Discipleship

Before we leave this pillar of discipleship, we must look at a few more key things Jesus said about discipleship and about the cost and conditions of becoming a disciple.

We read in Matthew 4 that Jesus came preaching, "Repent, for the kingdom of heaven is at hand" (verse 17), and calling out to men, "Follow me, and [in turn] I will make you fishers of men" (verse 19). Immediately they responded, left their fishing nets, their ship, and their father, and followed (verses 20-22). Immediately they reorganized their priorities. They didn't just talk about following. They counted the cost, cut ties, and did it. In fact, over the next sixty years, ten of these twelve disciples died a martyr's death because of their unfailing commitment to follow Christ.

The disciples did not know all of the cost when they began to follow. They had new opportunities all through the next years to choose to turn back or to follow on. Jesus spoke to them often of the need to give total allegiance to Himself if they were to be disciples:

- "Whosoever... shall confess me [unashamedly] before men, him will I confess before my Father... BUT whosoever shall deny me [be ashamed of me and of being identified as belonging to me] before men, him will I also deny before my Father" (Matthew 10:32-33, emphasis added).

- Jesus didn't come to bring peace on earth, but to call men and women to choices which divide like a sword, choices that will set a man at odds with his father, with his household (Matthew 10:34-36), choices that will lead to brother killing brother and parents delivering their children to be killed because they choose to confess Jesus in all of life (Matthew 10:21).

- "And ye shall be hated of all men for my name's sake; but he that endureth to the end shall be saved" (Matthew 10:22).

- "He that loveth father or mother more than me is *not worthy of me:* and [notice this next one which is very significant in our day when Grandpa and Grandma, and Dad and Mom are following the children instead of leading them]: he that loveth [honors and follows] son or daughter more than me is *not worthy of me*" (Matthew 10:37, emphasis added).

- And furthermore, "He that taketh not his cross and followeth after me [in my steps and life] is *not worthy of me*. He that findeth [or seeks to save and build up] his life shall lose it; and he that loseth his life for my sake shall find it" (Matthew 10:38-39, emphasis added).

- Luke 14:26 puts it this way, "If any man hate not his father and mother and wife . . . yea and his own life [his own will, his own right to be king and lord of his life] also, he *cannot be my disciple*." (emphasis added)

- "And whosoever doth not bear his cross [count the cost, prepare to suffer in this world, and deny himself] and come after me, *cannot be my disciple*" (Luke 14:27, emphasis added).

- "For which of you, intending to build a tower [which is something good], sitteth not down first and counteth the cost . . . so likewise, whosoever he be that forsaketh not all that he hath, he *cannot be my disciple*" (Luke 14:28-33, emphasis added).

Reevaluating Our Priorities in Light of Discipleship

These words and many others like them should tear at our hearts. How far short we fall! How we need to agonize and cry out. We need to be gripped with His call to be disciples and make disciples. We have been detoured into a focus on church services and attempts to build the church, which Jesus said He would do; it's His job, not ours. Furthermore, we have neglected the job *He* gave *us* to do—discipleship. If we will make disciples, fulfilling our part, I believe that He will build and unite the church.

Brothers, we must consider what in each of our churches is detouring us and keeping us from following this most basic command. We must stop and urgently consider the cost of entering into a life of kingdom discipleship. *What changes must we make in our personal and church life so that we can get back to what Jesus actually told us to be and to do?* What must be our message? What strategies could we purposefully implement to demonstrate to God our commitment to disciple-making? We need to discover afresh who we are, why we are here, and what pattern of biblical faithfulness we can follow in every area of life that can be passed on to our children, our converts, and the next generation. If we fail in this, we will have nothing to call people to, nothing to model, and nothing to pass on. Jesus said, "If ye continue [year after year and then generation after generation] in my word, then [and only then] are ye my disciples indeed" (John 8:31).

MEMORY AID

- Pillar 1—COMMUNION—**God exists**—I can know Him in sweet fellowship.

- Pillar 2—COMMUNICATION—**God has spoken**—I can hear Him and obey.

- Pillar 3—COMMUNITY—**Peoplehood**—I can be joined to His new nation.

- Pillar 4—CITIZENSHIP—**The Kingdom of God**—I can be part of His upside down kingdom right now.

- Pillar 5—COMMITMENT—**Discipleship**—I can count the cost and become an apprentice in the new community of the kingdom.

- Pillar 6—CONVERSION—**The New Birth**—In the next section we look at salvation, the doorway into the kingdom.

Seeds of the Faith—Pillar 6

The faith stands as mighty pillars, solid and unchanging. It rises as glorious mountain peaks, but it began its work in me as little seeds.

Some of you might be wishing you could have grown up in a liberal church like I did and then suddenly "seen the light." I also used to wish I had a wonderful testimony of being gloriously saved from a horrid life. But I didn't. I didn't even have a date written in my Bible to prove when I'd been born again.

I came to know Christ at camp (CFO) when I was about fifteen years old. Camp was the one week of the year that our family received spiritual food. We learned much of intimate relationship with Christ, of the quiet, Spirit-filled life, and of prayer, but there was no great focus on sin, repentance, or practical Christianity. My spiritual walk suffered because some of these foundational stones were not properly laid in my life. But now I see there was a blessing in it, too. From those early years, being a Christian involved a relationship with Christ in all of life and not just a past event and a date in my Bible.

I didn't know much. I didn't come to Christ in the "right" way, but somehow I came to know God and very slowly began saying yes to Him. I didn't do this because I was so good or because I prayed the right prayer, but because I had a new nature starting its work in me. A seed had been planted.

PILLAR 6

The New Birth

We believe it is the new covenant and the new birth that make kingdom living, holy peoplehood, and discipleship possible.

My dad always enjoyed mind puzzles. One of them went like this: "A man is in a room with two doors. One door leads to hell and one to heaven. At each door stands a guard. One guard can tell only the truth, and the other can tell only lies. You are allowed to ask just one question to help determine which door you will go through to get out of the room. What will your question be?"

The problem is that you don't know which guard is a liar, and if you ask the liar which door goes to heaven, he will point to the wrong door. The right question to ask is, "What would the other guard say is the door to heaven?" Then you should take the opposite door. If you ask this question to the liar, he will point out the door to hell. If you ask the truthful guard, he will also truthfully tell you what the liar would say and thus point to the door to hell, which is why you should take the other door!

That is an enjoyable exercise to work through with children to teach them how to think, but real life actually has two doors: one into the kingdom of God and one away from it. There also is much false information, or lies, about what is the right door into the kingdom. So what questions will you ask to find the right door and enter the kingdom?

The Door

- The kingdom (Pillar 4) is the overarching and eternal reality. It is God's eternal country, God's room.
- The new people (Pillar 3) are the subjects or citizens of that kingdom. They are His nation. They are the goal of all that He is doing,
- Discipleship (Pillar 5) is the tool and the teacher to get His people to spiritual maturity.

Pillar 6 will show us that the new birth is the door to get us into the kingdom country, into membership and citizenship with that people, and into the school of discipleship. Perhaps you think this pillar of the new birth should have been mentioned sooner. It is put here on purpose because in our day the emphasis is too often put upon the door (forgiveness of sins and conversion). Because of this misplaced emphasis, believers are many times left standing in the doorway instead of fully entering into the room of the kingdom, into the wide land of being all God intended us to be, which is true freedom.

So the good news of evangelism is not just that your sins can be forgiven, that you can accept Jesus into your heart, and that you can go to heaven. We cheat the new believer if we do not show them the deep communion, new society, kingdom citizenship and costly discipleship that are part of the salvation package.

Let us state it clearly: It is God Himself who has provided the "power to become the sons of God, even to them that believe on His name: which were born, not of blood, nor of the will of the flesh, nor of the will of man, but of God" (John 1:12-13). "Except a man be born again, he cannot see the kingdom of God" (John 3:3).

Natural Blindness and the New Birth

The kingdom of God existed from the beginning, but man could not see or experience it. It was beyond him. Man was born into the natural, earthly, sinful realm. He knew and even desired God and His commands, but he kept "falling short of the glory" and standard of God—which is sin (Romans 3:23). There was distance between man and God, this dark cloud of sin between them.

So God, as we already saw, said He would make a new covenant with His people—not like the old one in which the laws were on stone tablets outside of them, not like the old covenant in which His expectations became like a burden on their backs. But rather, He promised He would give His people a new heart, and a new mind. He would give His Spirit to work in His people, and would actually write His laws on their hearts. "And I will put my Spirit within you, and will cause you to walk in my statutes, and ye shall keep my judgments [my decisions about what is right] and do them" (Ezekiel 36:25-28; Jeremiah 32:38-40; Hebrews 8:10-11; Hebrews 10:16-17).

Man could not see the kingdom of God because he was born into the natural world. But now, God, through His Son Jesus, has made it possible for man to be born a second time, this time into the spiritual world. In other words, God has provided the way for man to become spiritually alive, to have a new supernatural nature—not like the old nature with which he was born. Let me stress again that this new nature is the work of God— this power to actually live as God's

Consequences
of Ignoring Pillar 6:

Results of life with no new nature:

- *The power of the fall and the old life continue to bind and blind man.*
- *He tries to do good with an old nature.*
- *He trusts in a date written in his Bible, a prayer he repeated, or the act of "joining church" to save him, but he has no clear, new life in Christ.*
- *His concern is to get to heaven, not to give himself unconditionally to God.*
- *His faith is one compartment of his life, but his life is still very much his own.*
- *The faith has never excited him, because he has actually never entered in through the door—Christ.*
- *Business, hockey, toys, clothes, Internet, family, and houses are what occupy his real thoughts and goals.*
- *He is in the church, but he has never been born again.*

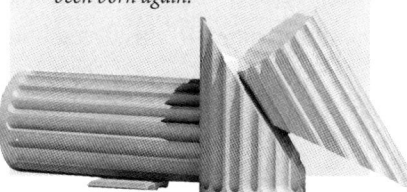

sons and daughters, to keep His desires and laws, comes only to those "born of God" (John 1:13).

A Dog in the Park

Think of the difference in nature between a dog and a man. The man walks through a park and admires the flowers, the statues, and the view. The dog sees none of this. He heads straight for the garbage can. Dogs see and value different things because they have different natures.

So it is with the believer and the unbeliever. A dog cannot change his nature and become like a man. But God made it possible that man, with an earth-bound nature and view of things, can be transformed by the Spirit of God so that he has a heaven-focused nature and view of things.

The man who is born a second time, this time spiritually, receives the nature of God (1 Corinthians 2:9-16; 2 Corinthians 3:14-18; 5:17, 21). He becomes "a partaker of the divine nature, having escaped [or made his exodus from] the corruption that is in the world through lust" (2 Peter 1:4).

When a new baby is born, we wonder what it will be like, what kind of nature it will have. So, too, with a new Christian we expectantly wait to see what God will do in this new creature!

Let us make some observations about this new spiritual life of the believer:

1. First, it is important that we fully acknowledge how far we have fallen. It is not just that we have a human, earthly nature, but more than that, we "were dead in trespasses and sins," and "walked according to the course of this world," and were influenced and ruled by "the prince of the power of the air." We lived "fulfilling the desires of the flesh and of the mind, and were by nature [note this] the children of wrath [the children who deserved God's wrath]" (Ephesians 2:1-3).

2. Related to this, we acknowledge that God's laws and desires are good, but we just cannot do them. "The law of sin which is in my members" is warring against that which is good—and wins (Romans 7:23; 8:2)! The "carnal [earth-bound] mind [that was

in me] is enmity against God [is God's enemy] for it is not subject [obedient] to the law of God, neither indeed can be. So then
they that are in the flesh cannot please God" (Romans 8:6-8).

3. What then is required? Jesus put it simply: "The time is fulfilled,
    and the kingdom of God is at hand; repent ye, and believe the gos-
    pel" (Mark 1:15). God "now commandeth all men everywhere to
    repent" (Acts 17:30). For, "If thou shalt confess with thy mouth the
    Lord Jesus, and shalt believe in thine heart that God raised him
    from the dead, thou shalt be saved" (Romans 10:9).

Pictures of Christ's Saving Work

What is it that Christ has done and that we are to believe in? What He
has accomplished already has been pictured as the new birth, in which
we receive a new nature. But the Scripture also has many other pictures
showing what happens when we become Christians. You might say that
salvation is like a many-sided house and photos have been taken from
different angles in attempts to capture the whole beauty of it.

Resurrection—Do you know anyone who can evade death? I once
managed a ranch for an elderly doctor who did not plan to die. He was
going to build a little cottage for me to retire in. My son was to take over
the ranch, and Doc planned to continue supervising from his chalet
which overlooked his land. All of his optimistic planning did not keep
Doc alive, and I have not heard of anyone else who can evade death.

Jesus also died. In fact, He predicted His own crucifixion. But what
demands our attention is not that He said He would not die, but something even more amazing. He claimed He would rise up from the dead
after three days (Mark 9:31; 10:32-34; Matthew 27:62-66; Luke 24:1-
8, 44-48). He would do this because He had the power over death and
hell. He said, "I am the resurrection and the life: he that believeth in me
though he were dead [and in the grave], yet shall he live [be resurrected
from the grave]" (John 11:25). Today we are so used to talk of the resurrection that we take it for granted. We can easily forget that Christ's
resurrection was history-making, earth-shattering, life-changing news.

The primary theme of the preaching about Christ in the book of Acts is that He has risen indeed and must be believed in for salvation. **He is the Victor!** In Him, sin, death, hell, and Satan are conquered. He said He would die and rise; and He did. All His doubting disciples testified that it happened (Acts 2:32). Then they gave their lives preaching that because He rose from the dead, we, too, can rise to newness of life and one day be resurrected from our grave with Him "whom God hath raised up, having loosed the pains of death: because it was not possible that He should be holden of it" (Acts 2:24).

These disciples "preached through Jesus the resurrection from the dead" (Acts 4:2, 33). Paul was put in prison, he says, for one reason—that he preached "the resurrection of the dead" (Acts 24:21). Peter testifies of our salvation, that we are born again "unto a lively hope by the resurrection of Jesus Christ from the dead" (1 Peter 1:3; Romans 8:11). He says that in baptism we present a visible picture of the resurrection of Jesus Christ, and a testimony of the good, clear conscience we have toward God, because we are saved by His resurrection (1 Peter 3:21).

Do you know anyone else who has raised himself from the grave? Today I read the obituary of a man who, his relatives claimed, had gone to "his eternal reward," but on what basis can they say that? Who can be so bold as to make such a statement? Or on what basis can you or I hope to be raised from our grave and given eternal life? I have no power to keep myself from the grave, and certainly none to get myself out of it. The only basis for my hope is that Christ is the Victor. In other words, the only safe place to be when I approach death is beside the One who has conquered death. If I believe in Him and am joined by faith to Him, I will share in His resurrection victory and life! This is the earliest picture of what Christ has done to save us and of what the Christians believed and preached. There are other pictures.

Redemption—As a lamb was slain at Passover, and as slaves were redeemed out of Egypt, so, too, Christ the Lamb of God (John 1:29, 36) was slain and has delivered us, has redeemed us, has been made a ransom and sacrifice for us. His life was offered up in our place. There was an exchange. He took our sin and, in turn, gave us His righteousness. He purchased us back from our slavery to sin and death. In accepting that, we become His possession! We are not freed to be our own, but to be His. He paid the price. "For Christ also hath once suffered for sins, the just for the unjust, that He might bring us to God" (1 Peter 3:18), and it is Christ "in whom we have redemption through His blood, the forgiveness of sins" (Ephesians 1:7). The important point in the discussion about redemption is that we have been purchased. We are never again to be our own.

Justification—This is similar to the preceding picture of redemption. "He who knew no sin was made to be sin for us that we might be made the righteousness of God in him" (2 Corinthians 5:21). Justification simply means that I am made righteousness. I am made right, made back into the way I am supposed to be. We have been "justified [made right] freely by his grace through the redemption that is in Christ Jesus" (Romans 3:24).

Reconciliation and peace—We who were separated from God are now made His friends. Now, "all things are of God, who hath reconciled us [brought us together] to

---

Blessings
of Embracing Pillar 6:

Benefits of the new birth:

- *The people God created have fallen, but in Christ there is a whole new beginning.*

- *God gives man a new nature, so what was not possible in the Old Testament is now possible.*

- *There is restoration, forgiveness, and new life.*

- *Christ's blood has brought peace between God and man, and between man and man.*

- *God's forgiven people are a picture of this real peace in a world of turmoil.*

- *Man's part is repentance and faith.*

- *By passing through the door of salvation, man is transferred into the kingdom of God.*

- *He is joined to God's new people.*

- *He enters into a life of discipleship and obedience.*

- *He is no longer his own. He is the purchased property of Christ.*

- *His ties to the world have been broken, and Christ is in charge.*

- *The decision has been made.*

- *He is at rest.*

- *All he does from now on is for the glory of Christ his Lord.*

himself by Jesus Christ and hath given to us the ministry of reconciliation" (2 Corinthians 5:18). "When we were enemies, we were reconciled to God by the death of His Son" (Romans 5:10) and, "Now in Christ Jesus ye who were... far off are made nigh by the blood of Christ. For He is our peace who hath made both one and hath broken down the middle wall of partition between us" (Ephesians 2:13-17).

We must ask an important question: Who were the enemies? They were the Gentiles. They were despised by the Jews and considered unclean. But now in Jesus, Jews and Gentiles are unified as one new man.

The Gospel makes peace between enemies. The Gospel commissions us to go into the world reconciling men to God and thus to each other. The Gospel is the Gospel of peace brought in by the Prince of Peace. Salvation introduces us to a kingdom of peace in which our King is pictured as a lamb, and in which the lion and lamb will one day lie down together. We, the church, are called to be the first fruits here and now of that peaceful kingdom (Isaiah 2:1-5; 9:1-7; 11:1-9). In Isaiah, the prophecies of the coming King go hand in hand with the vision of the peace of His kingdom!

Why is it critically important that we note this? It is because the doctrine of nonresistance in all of life is not some little addition that some churches add on as an extra belief, as a restriction or as an appendix. Again, I want you to note that I have not made a separate pillar for this doctrine because it is not something separate. It is an essential part of the very nature of salvation, and to remove it from the doctrine of salvation is to alter totally the whole nature of what salvation actually is. No; peace, reconciliation, and nonresistance are at the heart of what the Gospel is. The church in its first two hundred years knew no other option, for how can you make peace when you are aggressively striving, arguing, defending your property, or going to war?

This is a major area of difference with most evangelical churches. They cut out this vital aspect of the saving Gospel. But what about us? Do we really believe in nonresistance? Do we believe in it for all of life? Do we believe in it in church life? Do we live a Gospel of reconciliation, or are we, too, those who preach it well, but fail in the living of it? This, of course, is the great challenge. Remember, it is the costly living of the Gospel of peace that makes us radical believers, not just having it in our statement of faith.

More Erroneous Concepts of Salvation

Consider a couple of other errors in many modern concepts of salvation:

1. The first common error is believing that a person can be legally declared righteous or holy or sanctified and yet never demonstrate the fruit and reality of righteousness, holiness, or sanctification. Some speak of our position in Christ. They see themselves seated with Him in heaven, but it seems to have little bearing on how they live.

   In practical terms, this means that…

   - The one redeemed from sin and forgiven will *forgive others;* if not, we question whether a new spirit is in him.

   - The one justified and made righteous *will be more and more righteous in life,* for righteousness leads to righteousness. Any other crop of fruit will cause us to question the nature of the tree.

   - The one reconciled to God *will be a peacemaker,* because God extended him peace when he was an enemy and an alien.

   This is the Gospel of salvation. It is not just about what Jesus did, but about what He is doing in you and me. The Gospel is about how we actually live, not just about what we claim to believe. Salvation is not just "the door." It is the "room" beyond.

2. A second error is that we may have prayed a prayer, put up our hand, walked to an altar, asked Jesus into our heart as a child, or been baptized into the church with our peers, but we have no evidence in our lives that we have become spiritually alive and have become "partakers of the divine nature" (2 Peter 1:4).

3. Thirdly, we may have been taught that if we did pray one of these prayers, did get baptized, or did try to walk with God for a time, we should never question our salvation. Many with no experience of Christ's life, victory, and holiness are cheated from receiving true salvation in Christ because others try to assure them that they have done all they need to do. Don't just listen to others. Either you have the inner witness of resurrection life and righteousness or you don't. At all costs, get it.

More Pictures of Salvation

Let's get back to the images of salvation that we have been seeing in God's Word. Remember, these are like viewing different angles of the same house or different pictures of the same reality. We have seen already the following:

- The New Birth (Picture a newborn baby—"I wonder what it will be like?")
- Resurrection (Picture the first-century world hearing the news for the first time ever.)
- Redemption (Picture the Lamb of God being sacrificed to purchase you.)
- Justification (Picture something fixed and better than it was before.)
- Reconciliation/Peace (Picture bitter enemies embracing.)

Two other beautiful pictures are these:

Union with Christ—(Picture a wedding.) Think of the phrases "in Christ" and "Christ in me." These phrases, so often used by Paul, show the vital connection of Christ and the believer. We are "created in Christ Jesus" (Ephesians 2:10; 2 Corinthians 5:17; John 15). All the "spiritual blessings in heavenly places" are available to us "in Christ" (Ephesians 1:3). On the other hand, we can also say, "I am crucified with Christ: nevertheless I live; yet not I, but Christ liveth in me" (Galatians 2:20).

The inner witness of the Spirit—(Picture a child excited to see Daddy.) We said that under the new covenant, God gives us a new heart and His own Spirit to make possible what was impossible under the old covenant. Ephesians 1:13 says, "After that ye believed, [then] ye were sealed with that Holy Spirit of promise." Paul says much about this Holy Spirit in Romans 8. For instance, "The Spirit is life" in you (verse 10), and "Ye have received the Spirit of adoption, whereby we cry, Abba [Daddy], Father. The Spirit itself beareth witness with our spirit that we are the children of God" (Romans 8:15-16). Look also at Romans 8:2: It is "the law of the Spirit of life in Christ Jesus" that is now working in the believer and setting him free from that old "law of sin and death." There is a new ruling influence and power in the believer's life that makes it possible for him or her to fulfill the law and desires of Jesus.

What a rich salvation!

MEMORY AID

- Pillar 1—COMMUNION—**God exists**—Intimate relationship now.
- Pillar 2 —COMMUNICATION—**God has spoken**—Hear and obey now.
- Pillar 3—COMMUNITY—**Peoplehood**—God's distinct and holy nation now.
- Pillar 4—CITIZENSHIP—**The Kingdom of God**—Citizenship in the kingdom and "country" governed by God's heavenly laws, beginning now.
- Pillar 5—COMMITMENT—**Discipleship**—Called to be disciples and make disciples now.
- Pillar 6—CONVERSION—**The New Birth**—The supernatural inner working of God that makes possible all that God designed and intended for His kingdom people now.
- Pillar 7—CONFESSION—**Faith**—Missing this essential pillar will keep us from the doorway of salvation and from the life of victory in the land.

Seeds of the Faith—Pillar 7

The faith stands as mighty pillars, solid and unchanging. It rises as glorious mountain peaks, but it began its work in me as little seeds.

Seeds of faith? They have been planted so many ways in my life. They are still being planted. Without faith, it is impossible to please God. Every pillar we've discussed in this book requires the planting of seeds of faith. Every day I go forth with living faith. Once I was young with a very busy faith. Today I am older, and my body is breaking down before its time. I must sit much more. I have faced failure and disappointment, but in all these things, new seeds of faith keep being planted. At every stage of life, I live by faith.

It was on a Sunday night in the first year of our marriage that I sat down with my wife Laura and told her I felt God was calling me to leave ranching and go into the ministry. I thought I was crazy, but as we began to talk, it became clear that God had been at work throughout my whole life preparing me for this moment. Not only that, God had been at work in Laura that very night. Earlier, she had asked if she could stay home and seek God that Sunday night instead of joining me at the evening service. This had never happened before, but I relented and went to church alone. Hours later, as we sat together, she told me God had impressed upon her heart that very night that He was going to change the whole direction of our lives and that it was okay. She could trust Him. Those were faith-building moments that we have looked back to many times.

I wish I could tell you about the multitudes of times since then that God has provided and directed. For Laura and me, life has been filled with steps of obedience that seemed impossible, and of going out, literally "not knowing where." None of this has been easy. The great faith booster has been seeing that as we take tiny little steps of obedience, we discover that God is at work, doing more than we could ever ask or think or imagine.

Faith is more than God directing and providing. Faith demands action from me. I demonstrate my faith in God's ability by obeying, by doing what He calls me to do, even if it goes against my flesh. A very important seed was planted for this life of faith during my high school years at St. John's. I learned to act; I learned to obey orders; I learned to discipline my body. I came to love the challenges of life. I began to see that what others thought of as impossible was not impossible at all. Mountains were things to be conquered, and giants were enemies to be slain. I learned that I could paddle a canoe ten hours a day for three weeks. I could snowshoe in the dark for five hours every Wednesday all winter, and I could obey orders and get schoolwork done on time or suffer the painful consequences.

At St. John's, I learned to discipline my body and to obey even when it seemed impossible. I thank God for that important seed.

PILLAR 7

Faith

We believe the land of promise and fulfillment is entered and possessed by faith. Faith sees what God wants to do and does it.

How much do you know of living each day by faith? A dear brother and I once visited a group of people that were lost in deep darkness, although very religious. As we visited, one of the boys came in and told his mother he was off to the gravel pit with some of the others to get drunk. The poor ladies present there just cackled, but my spirit grieved.

I entered into a conversation with that young man and the ladies about the Bible, drunkenness, anger, immorality, and all the abuse that comes with a lifestyle of drinking. They fully recognized the horrible fruit in their lives, but unanimously declared that it was impossible to have it any other way.

There is no possible victory, they said, over fleshly passions and anger: "The way we are today is the way our fathers were twenty years ago and the way it will be twenty years from now. The important thing is that we stay in the church."

So does faith have anything to do with overcoming anger, bitterness, pornography, selfishness, and our other vices? Can you actually be saved from your sin? (Matthew 1:21).

In the previous discussions we have seen something of God's open arms, of His design for a people for whom He is King, of the cost of becoming a part of that people and kingdom, and finally of the pictures God has given us showing us what must happen for a person to be born into that new race.

Now it is time for the question: Do you believe? Will you reach out in faith and accept what God has prepared and offered to you? Some of you may need to kneel down and repent specifically of your sin and by faith receive true forgiveness and salvation unto eternal life in the Lord Jesus. Others of you are already in the door to the land, but you have forgotten the faith that got you in at the beginning, so you keep doubting and failing when you meet giants in the land. Only by faith did the men of old overcome great giants and obstacles.

Again, let me ask some of you seasoned pilgrims how much you know of actually walking by faith? I will never forget the account of a man somewhere in the area of the Czech Republic who worked long hours in the coal mines, but each evening after supper, he would go out his door and say, "God, I only have these few short hours to do something for you. I don't have time to waste, so please lead me directly to some soul who needs ministry." Night after night God led him to the very door where he was needed. Is that just for him? No! It can be and has been our experience, but all too often it is the exception instead of the norm.

We often sense divine leading at the start of some great work of God and then settle down into "regular" church life. Do you and I as individuals and brotherhoods really want to pay the cost of engaging in a walk of faith into the unknown? Is this kind of life just for a few people and a few churches, or is it meant to be normal Christian living and normal church life?

Is it possible that we are missing something of the great adventure of stepping out in a life of faith because we don't think God could really use or lead us? Have we just accepted that the way it is today in my life and ministry is the way it will be in twenty years?

Without Faith We Have Nothing

Without faith we cannot please Him (Hebrews 11:6). Moses' faith inspired a huge nation of slaves to flee the land of Egypt against incredible odds. They passed through the Red Sea on dry land and turned around to watch that same sea come rushing in to destroy their enemies. Tragically, just months later, doubt and evil reports caused a whole generation of Israelites to shrivel up in fear and choose death in the wilderness instead of entrance to the land of promise (Numbers 13-14). That same fear and doubt can also destroy our generation today, causing us to go astray. Why settle for doubt, mediocrity, and wilderness living when by faith we could take the land and the giants?

We have seen some incredible promises of all that God has for us and also some wonderful commands and laws that help all of life to work right. For instance we have seen:

> *Consequences*
> *of Ignoring Pillar 7:*
>
> *Results of not walking by faith:*
> - *Life has no grand purpose.*
> - *I am trying to be good, but there has been no deep inner change in me.*
> - *I see life through little human eyes.*
> - *I can't identify with those who joyfully submit and worship.*
> - *I struggle to believe that God is at work.*
> - *I am not sure if He can use me.*
> - *I don't obey God because I am afraid of what others will think.*
> - *I doubt that God will actually guide us as a brotherhood.*
> - *I am full of worries about money, health, crops, business, children, and the future.*
> - *I see all the problems in myself or in others.*
> - *My life is filled with the things of this world, and seeking God is not in first place.*

- That God wants His own people on earth.

- That those people are citizens of His kingdom and not the kingdom of this world.

- That the blessings and riches of our heritage as His people demands that we be separated from the lusts of our flesh and from the world.

Faith and Facts

Those three statements are some simple facts that God has revealed to us. Every Christian in some way has heard these facts, but what do we do with them? Do we just talk about them (a museum- or lecture-hall-type of faith), or do we apply them and obey? Do we enter the land or go in more wilderness circles?

We have seen:

- That Christ died in our place
- That I, as a Christian, died with Him, to lust, anger, and self-will, among other things
- That Christ rose from the dead so that sin's power could be broken and I could be forgiven, reconciled to God and to man

These are the *facts*, and there are so many more:

- I am in Christ and He is in me.
- Apart from Him, I can do nothing.
- All my service is nothing if it doesn't flow from an inner life of faith and communion with God.

Faith takes hold of these facts and acts on them. Faith sees them as living reality.

The Key is Faith

So you see that the key that brings us to Christ, the door of salvation, is *faith*. The key to walking into the land of the kingdom is *faith*. The essential key to victory over sin, to a fruitful life, to godly homes, to obedience in small things and large, to following God's will, and to Spirit-filled life and ministry, is *faith*.

Think again of Israel at the Jordan River (Numbers 13; Joshua 1-4). They came there on two different occasions.

The first time they doubted and lost the right to go in. Do you think that they wanted to live in the wilderness for forty more years? No. They possessed the wilderness as their home only because they did not act on the promises and commands of God.

The second time they came, they faced the same facts, the same giants, the same promises. The only difference was that the second time they believed and acted. They did not have to pray a lot to enter and take the land! They had to obey a lot, and as they, by faith, obeyed, God gave them the victory and the land as their new home.

Faith is the victory that overcomes the world, the flesh, and the devil. Many people have all the *facts*, but only a few, only a small remnant—the serious disciples—will take the land of promise by *faith*.

A confession of the faith is so much more than something written in point form in a little book. It is something that must flow out of my heart, be spoken by my mouth, and be continually written on my life.

Blessings
of Embracing Pillar 7:

Benefits of walking by faith:

- Life is an adventure.
- My nature, my mind and my eyes are changed.
- I now see life through spiritual eyes.
- I go forth expecting doors of ministry and witness to open.
- I call others to discipleship and obedience because I know it works.
- We gather as brothers and expect God to direct through His Word and prayer.
- I seek His kingdom first and trust Him to supply all that is needed.
- I am mocked for making godly decisions and denying my flesh.
- I separate myself from ungodly influences because I love God.
- I share all I have with God's people and make it available for His work, because what I have is not mine.
- I am confident that God is in control.
- I trust Him to work in me and others.
- I do the little that I can but believe He is working in greater ways than I could ever know.
- I rejoice and give thanks because God is good, and His ways are excellent.

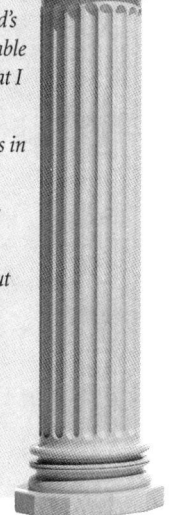

Therefore, if we are to experience continuing life in the land, that is, in God's kingdom, we need:

1. A life of *continuing* faith. Faith is a part of everything in the physical world and the spiritual world. You go to the store because you believe you will find groceries there. You plant a seed and believe that it will grow. You kick a ball and believe that it will fly high and then drop. By faith you act on the facts you know. So, too, by faith, you act on all God has revealed. *You will never graduate* from living by faith and being tested and matured in your faith. This leads us to the next pillar and to the second thing that is essential if we are to have *continual* life in Christ.

2. A life of *continual* humility and dying. *We have not arrived.* We press forward to the mark of the high calling of God in Christ Jesus (Philippians 3:14). We, like the churches in Revelation 2-3, need to keep hearing "what the Spirit is saying to the churches" and to keep repenting where we fall short.

Memory Aid

Read over each of the pillar titles and try to remember what you have learned about each of them.

- Pillar 1—COMMUNION—
- Pillar 2—COMMUNICATION—
- Pillar 3—COMMUNITY—
- Pillar 4—CITIZENSHIP—
- Pillar 5—COMMITMENT—
- Pillar 6—CONVERSION—**The New Birth**—The supernatural inner working of God that makes possible all that God designed and intended for His kingdom people now.
- Pillar 7—CONFESSION—**Faith**—Missing this essential pillar will keep us from the doorway of salvation and from the life of victory in the land.
- Pillar 8—CROSS-BEARING—**Humility**—Continual confession is both a positive expression of our faith in God, as we just saw, and a negative expression of our own great sin, weakness, and need.

Seeds of the Faith—Pillar 8

The faith stands as mighty pillars, solid and unchanging. It rises as glorious mountain peaks, but it began its work in me as little seeds.

I left all my earthly ambitions to go into the ministry—and I loved it. It was my life. But we had clearly sensed God calling us apart to seek a clearer understanding of His design for the Christian life and church. For my wife, life carried on much as before. She was a busy, fulltime mother and teacher; but I was struggling. All that I lived for had been stripped away. I had no purpose. I found myself failing terribly as a dad, a husband, and a Christian. But, there was one constant, one thing that never changed, and that was God.

In our second winter of retreat in the Rockies I began to go to the barn loft to pray. Then in the summer, up on a hill surrounded by moss, ferns, and big fir and cedar trees, I dug holes and put in railroad ties for pillars. I built a platform. Then walls and rafters went up. I split cedar shakes for the siding and roof and salvaged birch flooring for the interior walls. We found some antique windows and doors, and my wife made curtains. My father-in-law gave me an old fireplace, and finally I had my prayer cabin.

It took a few years to build the cabin, but that didn't matter. You see, the whole process was an act of prayer. As I built, I was crying out to God. When the platform was erected, I went there to pray. When the framing was done, I took a table up there and started lighting the fire to keep warm as I studied my Bible. Now my point here is simply this—I was at my lowest point. There was nothing left. I had only God. I was dependent on Him alone. Unless He came through, I was finished. I look back and realize that was just where God wanted me—at a place of humility and brokenness. Not only that, it was where He wants me all the time.

I find the ground of humility when I live in the place of total dependence on God.

Years have passed and white hair has found a welcome resting place upon my head. I've experienced seasons of true fulfillment, of growth, and of disappointment. I have seen great and small men falter, great churches and movements shaken, popular books and programs fade into oblivion. Men who have served are set aside. Ones who have sacrificed are misunderstood. Offenses come, followed by forgiveness and healing. I have observed the "quiet in the land" and seen pride. I have watched the soft and meek personality cave in and fail to obey God. What then is humility?

Is it first about my relationship to man and how I appear to man? Or is rooted in my relationship to God? It is in the lowest times of life, when I am alone, when all has failed and I am undone, that I have the clearest view of what humility is. It is there that I am left with nothing but God.

PILLAR 8

Humility

We believe we are to be continual living sacrifices who put our lives on the altar and die daily.

That is, we believe in the crucified life and in sharing in the sufferings of our Lord.

As Christians, we choose to accept the trials and sufferings that come our way. We, in some sense, see them as coming from God. As an earthly example of this, think of the beloved psalmist, David. He was just an old-covenant believer, and yet he had such a trust in God that he would not fight against King Saul who was seeking to kill him.

Years later when David was king, his own son Absalom arose to take the throne from him. David, instead of fighting, quietly left town. Along the way, Shimei, a descendant of King Saul, came out and cursed David and threw stones at him. But notice David's response: "Let him alone, and let him curse; for the Lord hath bidden him. It may be that the Lord will look on my affliction, and that the Lord will requite [repay] me good for his cursing this day" (2 Samuel 16:11-12).

What a testimony! No wonder David is so loved. His responses were not weakness or cowardice. They were true power, born out of a life that knew God and had totally surrendered to Him. David was the one who was right but did not fight to prove it. He rather saw himself as in need of correction from God. He bore the pain.

First the Cross

Salvation is the beginning of spiritual life. But please note: *Salvation began with a cross and ended with resurrection, life, and victory.* So, too, for us. It is *first the cross and **then** the glory.* We do not "arrive" in this life. Continually we face new levels of testing and pruning. Facing these new challenges requires continual humility, confession, and submission to the will of God. We daily take up our cross and die. We recognize and confess our humanness, our smallness, our ignorance, our failures, our sins, and our needs, both as individuals and as churches. We continually and sincerely confess these and pray for one another. God's blessing comes not on the great of the earth but on the contrite, poor, and needy.

Three Scriptures impacted me along these lines as a young believer. The first time I read the account of Isaiah seeing the holiness of God, it was as if I were there, as if I had just seen God and then seen myself: "Woe is *me* for *I* am undone; because *I* am a man of unclean lips, and *I* dwell in the midst of a people of unclean lips: for *mine* eyes have seen the King, the Lord of hosts" (Isaiah 6:5 emphasis added).

Then there was 2 Chronicles 7:14: "If My people, which are called by my name, shall humble *themselves*, and pray, and seek my face, and turn from *their* wicked ways; then will I hear from heaven, and will forgive their sin, and will heal their land." I saw that healing of the land (the specific country or place where we live) begins with the church meeting God and confessing her own sin. How easy it is to see the sin of the land, the sin of others; but God said the road to healing begins by allowing His finger to come down on my life, and on our lives as His church. To see healing and revival in our land demands our continual humility and confession.

The third Scripture was Revelation 2-3, in which the risen Jesus spoke to seven churches that had experienced firsthand the glories spoken of in the book of Acts, but in the letters written to them just a few years later only one of the seven heard a "Well done." Each of the other six churches was shown areas in which she needed to repent and hear what the Spirit of God was saying. If not, her very right to be a church would be taken away.

When I first discovered these Scriptures, I was part of a Pentecostal denomination riding on the coattails of a great revival in the past. They, like so many of us, were faced with many problems, yet still somehow saw themselves as the "right" church. I read Revelation 2-3 and again was undone. Here was the answer. We don't need to hold up our rightness and cover up our wrongness. We need to lay down our rightness, confess our need, and open our ears to God's voice. That voice might even be speaking to us through a person or church group we have looked down on.

When I excitedly reported what I had found in the Word, it produced no response. What I had just discovered, they had heard so many times before that they were somewhat immunized against the message. They felt it didn't really apply to them.

Don't shake your head. What about us? Which road are we as churches known for: the road of humility or the road of pride?

There is nothing easy or natural about any of this. If we are to live this supernatural life of humility, confession, and obedience to the Spirit, we must never stop lovingly calling each other back to this path of cross-bearing and joyful suffering. Martyrs are still needed

Consequences
of Ignoring Pillar 8:

When humility is missing:

- *Our faith becomes a cold tradition.*
- *We cover over our sin.*
- *We justify ourselves and blame others.*
- *We protect the good name of the church instead of confessing failures.*
- *Our children reject the faith and call us hypocrites.*
- *We defend our point of view and our position at all costs.*
- *We strive and disagree and wonder why God doesn't answer our prayers.*
- *God stops speaking because we don't obey anyhow.*
- *Our mission endeavors fail because there are walls between believers.*
- *It is obvious that we do not see God.*

in the church—living martyrs who are willing to die instead of making others die.

I Die

Do you remember who Christ came for? It was for others, for the poor, the sick, the outcast, the humble, those who saw their need. He did not come for the rich and self-sufficient.

Modern life has exalted the happiness of the individual as the chief goal of life. It has lifted up success, self-advancement, self-love, and self-gratification. These pursuits are contrary to the *crucified life*. They react against or reject the suffering of the cross in the believer's life.

Here and now, we are called to suffer. That means we are to die to self, including self-rule, self-satisfaction, and all the other self-infatuations. Perhaps in a future day we will be called on to die a literal martyr's death. We may die as martyrs later, but right now we are *living sacrifices*. Our bodies, our feelings, our ambitions, and our possessions are already surrendered up to death. We have already separated ourselves from the present evil world. We already have a home somewhere else, and that affects all we do. It affects how we live and how we die. I *die now* so I do not need to die eternally later. I *die* to my flesh and to the world, and in so doing, I find everlasting life. If I choose to seek the world and the life of the present age, then I, by my choice, lose an entrance to God's eternal world. I will find myself in the wilderness of death and hell forever.

Four Ways to Die

Here are four ways we can put our lives on the altar now:

- **In service**—My time, my passions, my gifts, my dollars, my personal space are given over to God and others.

- **In self-surrender**—"Not my will but thine" is my constant attitude. I do not seek my good, but the good of my brothers.

- **In stillness**—I can wait. When I want to react, I can say nothing because I give it to God. I do not need to defend myself. I do not need to respond. I can rest in God's presence. All my activity will not bring in God's kingdom; it may destroy it. Until I am at rest, I can be of no use to God or His people.

- **In simplicity**—I don't know very much. God pressed the "limit switch"—likely at the Tower of Babel—and the smartest of us know very little even in the areas of our specialties.

Years ago, I read of a genius in the 1800s named Tesla. He created thunder and lightning storms in the Arizona desert, operated electric lights without switches, designed a totally radio-controlled navy for the United States during their war with the Spanish (incidentally, they lacked the faith to build it) and much more. He understood electricity and realized that it was everywhere. It seems his limit switch in that area never got set. To this day, many of his theories and inventions are apparently held secret by the United States government, because no one alive is able to understand them.

Brothers, this simple report is a reminder to me of how very little I know. God installed a limit switch for a reason. So I must *die to what I think I know* and walk humbly before God and man.

He *alone* is my life. I lose my life in this world and find it again *in Him*.

> ## Blessings
> ### of Embracing Pillar 8:
>
> *Benefits of a life of humility:*
>
> - *We see God.*
> - *Our continual confession leads to a continual overflow of life.*
> - *Our continual openness and obedience opens the door for God to speak.*
> - *We seem to lose now, but in the end we inherit the land.*
> - *We make peace, not war.*
> - *We seek to edify instead of debating and striving about words.*
> - *We can pray without wrath and dissension because we are at peace.*
> - *We can stand against the enemy because he cannot divide us with pride, bitterness, or offense.*
> - *We know the joy of serving.*
> - *We have found the freedom of submitting.*
> - *We know that dying leads to life.*
> - *Simplicity marks our life.*

Looking Ahead

With the next pillar, we consider a very practical subject, one that we can only introduce. It is a pillar that must be in place or we will experience much confusion, strife, ineffectiveness and evil speaking. The practical shape of this pillar may vary from church to church, but it must be present, and it must be defined.

We have already seen that God has called us through the new birth to enter His new society—the community of the heavenly King. However, it is also important to understand that God also has given us a new order or a new government. The church involves both:

- Spirit and life (new birth, discipleship, faith, humility, etc.)

- Order (form, structure, and government)

It is important that we understand how we govern ourselves in the new society of God's people. It is important that we know—

- How we relate to each other

- What our responsibilities are

- What the lines of authority and accountability are

Every country and every family has a way that it orders and governs itself to promote a harmonious and fruitful life. Of course, we know that some countries and families have unclear, tyrannical, chaotic, or evil governing structures, but they all have some form of structure. Likewise, we believe that God has established some biblical boundaries, some perimeters and principles, for the governing of local churches and of His people.

That is what is ahead in this discussion. We are about to shift our focus to this very practical topic, but first I think it would be good to review and put together the spiritual pieces of the puzzle we have examined so far.

MEMORY AID

- Pillar 1—C_____—**God exists**—God in the very core of His nature is a relational being. He has always desired and worked toward an intimate relationship with man. That was why He created the world, why we still exist, and why He sent His Son and His Spirit to make it possible for us to know Him.

- Pillar 2—C_____—**God has spoken**—You cannot have a vital and close relationship if no one talks. But God has spoken in so many ways. For instance, He has spoken as our Creator, our King, our Savior, and our Father. Think of the close relationship Jesus had with His Father. The Bible says that they were one. They were so close that Jesus saw what His Father was doing (intending) and did it; He heard what His Father was saying and said it. That oneness is what God has designed and intended for us, so that we, too, can see what God is planning, hear what He is saying, and then act accordingly—obey.

- Pillar 3—C_____—**Peoplehood**—God desired that all men would freely choose to be His people, but man kept resisting God and choosing his own independent ways. God began His search for a people with Adam. He continued his search with Noah, then Abraham, and now with His Son, Jesus Christ. God has now given His own Spirit to the church so that they might be a minority, prophetic, alternative people group that models the intimate relational life and nature of heaven here on the earth. This is what Jesus prayed for in His last great prayer (John 17). It is what He still is praying for today despite all our failures. It is this people, this spotless bride, that Jesus has said He will come back to claim. He has not given up, and neither should we.

- Pillar 4—C_____—**The Kingdom of God**—This alternative people created by God are the subjects of a whole new visible nation—the kingdom of God. This kingdom is governed by the "upside down" laws of the life of heaven. The very nature of this kingdom sets it at variance with the kingdom and nations of this world, with the flesh, and with the devil. The opposing nature and laws of these two kingdoms make it biblically incomprehensible that anyone could be a dual citizen of both kingdoms. The true Christian has shifted his allegiance and his place of belonging. If we miss this reality of being the distinct kingdom people of God, our lives as Christians and churches will suffer great confusion and loss.

- Pillar 5—C_____—**Discipleship**— The thing that makes this alternative people distinct is that they are attempting to follow Jesus' pattern of living, and they are committed to calling others to follow as well. They are seeking in all of life to discover what God intended, what way of living and decisions would best line up with His nature and commandments, and thus what would present a godly option in place of the typical life of this world. Choosing this option is a very costly matter that has caused many to lose their families, their possessions, and even their lives.

- Pillar 6—C_____— **The New Birth**— This serious and costly life of following Jesus as His new kingdom people is not possible unless man's rebellious, independent, and hardened heart is taken out and replaced by the new nature, heart, and Spirit of God. Salvation is the door by which we are joined to Christ in His death, burial, and resurrection. It is the door by which we are given access to all that God has planned for His people.

- Pillar 7—C_____ — **Faith**—Faith is the key that opens the door so that we can be joined to Christ, to His kingdom, to His people, and to His new nature. Without faith, it is impossible to please God, impossible to continue living victoriously in His kingdom. Faith is to the spiritual life what breathing is to physical life.

- Pillar 8—CROSS-BEARING—**Humility** —The cost of following Christ and receiving His continuing life never stops. If we are to have continual revival and life, we must continually acknowledge our sin, our smallness, and our need. We must continually be ready to suffer hardship, rejection, and pain for His Name's sake. We must die to self and to our own life, and instead give our life for others. "First the cross and then the glory" was the pattern of Jesus' life, and it will be the pattern of life for those who wish to follow in His steps as His kingdom people.

- Pillar 9 —CHURCH—**Ecclesia**—We have just summarized the spiritual foundation of our life as serious followers of Jesus, our identity as His people, our place of belonging in His kingdom, and our mandate to model the life of heaven here on earth. Now we turn to the practical matter of how we are biblically to order and govern ourselves as the new society of God's people, how we are to order our life together in such a way that it honors and is consistent with the value that God places on both intimate relationships and our distinct separation as His holy people.

After that, we will consider the task we as His people have been given to do, the opposition we will face, and finally, the account we will one day give to God.

****

Why not try reviewing the first eight pillars in your head while you are driving, on paper, or even in your prayers?

Seeds of the Faith—Pillar 9

The faith stands as mighty pillars, solid and unchanging. It rises as glorious mountain peaks, but it began its work in me as little seeds.

One of the great influences in my life was my father-in-law. In the 1970s, many books were written on renewal of the church, and Dad had a lot of them. We would sit in his living room and each read our own book until some thought got our attention, and then we would launch into a long talk about the future of the church.

In those years, it was clear that the church was in great need of renewal. My own bookshelves filled up with titles about the church, and my mind overflowed with desire to see the church truly be the church.

Somehow, through all the reading and thoughts and dreams, something stood out. Jesus had prayed, "Thy kingdom come on earth as it is in heaven." He had a plan in heaven, and He wanted His people to give themselves to hearing His plan. He said, "Where two or three of you are together in the total interest of My Name alone you will be able to know My will and carry it out on earth" (Matthew 18:20, paraphrase).

It's not too hard for man to plan programs, to share ideas, or to fill church pews. But a great and costly seed was planted in me—a longing not just for good ideas or great services, but for a people who would together discern God's will and then do it.

PILLAR 9

Ecclesia

We believe the church, the ecclesia, is a worshiping community, ordered and governed as a brotherhood or body of equal members, under the headship of Jesus Christ.

Man has a longing for community, for belonging, for family. As we have talked in the previous pillars about these subjects we have attempted to establish what is called our *identity*—who we are. But any experience of community demands structure and order or it will turn into confusion and chaos, causing trust to be lost. This governing structure and agreement is what is called our *polity*.

Polity (*polis* is the Greek word for city; *politics* is the governing of the city) deals with everything related to *how we relate, organize, and govern ourselves within our group* and also *how we relate to those outside our group* such as overseers, a parent church, sister churches and new mission churches.

I recently read of a new church movement that in its pioneer years had its identity largely established. Its members knew who they were and what they wanted to do, but they kept running into problems until they defined their polity. Their belief is that a sound and sustainable church requires a defined and accepted polity *as well as* a defined and accepted identity.

In this section we will look at seven different aspects of the polity, or governing structure and program of the church. Polity is not an end in itself. It is a tool, a servant to help us get the job done.

An Urgent Question

As I have talked to people from Mennonite and other Germanic church backgrounds, it has become obvious that there is a lot of fear concerning this topic of the church and her leaders. In the early years of my search for direction, I noticed that in the messages, hymns, and conversation of people in these backgrounds, there seemed to be an emphasis on the church—so much so that I got the impression that the church had replaced God, and that the critical thing was what the church says, not what God says. And who was the church? It seemed it was the conference of ministers.

Needless to say, this was foreign to me, and I reacted against it. But can I frankly say that here I am years later, fellowshipping with people who have left these backgrounds, and I am wondering: Are we all reacting? Are we all afraid of the church, of leadership, of structure, of authority? How will this turn out?

A minister shared in a meeting that we will never be able to discuss and agree on matters of church doctrine and structure because of the authoritarian backgrounds we come from. A dear brother from another loosely-knit fellowship said his people are deathly afraid of authority. A Bible teacher systematically presented every biblical statement about eldership, and afterwards people protested, saying, "That is just his opinion."

This matter of the government and structure of the church and of groups of churches is a volatile subject. Fabien De Freitas, in his penetrating analysis of so-called independent churches, has suggested that perhaps we are actually just plagued with an independent spirit and a fear of having anyone tell us what to do. He has termed this a "my God and my Bible" attitude. In my own overstated words, some of his questions could be:

How can independent, unconnected groups of people, often lacking empowered leaders and clear direction, and interpreting the Bible as they individually see fit—call themselves the church? Doesn't the church have more authority than that? Isn't it part of something bigger than just our little local split? Doesn't it have defined beliefs, leaders, and even bishops who have authority to say no?

De Freitas takes this a step further and suggests that revival movements fall short of the characteristics required in order to be a church. A *movement* is something that is fluid, unstructured, undefined, and non-denominational, and that exerts its influence upon many religious backgrounds. With these characteristics in mind, is it possible that some of us are just part of revival *movements,* and that our reluctance to define more clearly what we believe and to define our governing and authority structure has kept us from establishing strong, sustainable churches?

So then, whereas on the one hand many are fleeing from authority, this brother is claiming to see the need for it and questioning if we can truly be the church without it (Fabien De Freitas, *Finding Church*).

Consequences
of Ignoring Pillar 9:

Results of dysfunctional ecclesia:

- *There is confusion instead of clarity.*
- *Individuals are unwilling to accept the idea of making decisions together.*
- *Decision making is a battle of wills.*
- *We don't know how to make clear decisions.*
- *What the minister or group decides is disregarded if I don't agree.*
- *We lack the clarity to bind and loose.*
- *It is hard to disciple, discipline, or plant churches.*
- *Ecclesia is not possible because there is not commitment.*
- *We are afraid of authority and of clearly defining what we believe.*
- *Meetings lack purpose, so members are discouraged and may not attend.*
- *The church becomes a hierarchy.*
- *Ministers feel discouraged and alone.*
- *We all have our own way, but complain because there is no love and no fellowship.*

It is easy to write off our critics, but one thing is clear. This matter of the doctrine of the church is something we must determine to examine more closely. So far, I have tried to paint a panoramic picture of God's kingdom purposes and people. Incidentally, I am not the only one who has been seeking to emphasize this vision. I believe it is God who has been laying it upon the hearts of His people, especially in these last few years. It seems to me that the Spirit of God emphasizes different truths at different times, to bring us slowly back to the fullness of His original purpose. In light of this, I want you to stop and prepare yourself to ask some timely questions as we go into these next sections of discussion:

- Is it possible that the challenge of this present hour for us as Anabaptist and Radical Believers' Churches is to relearn what God actually intends for the church?

- Could it be that we are failing practically to live out the vision of God's kingdom (as outlined in the previous pillars) *because we have not* yet correctly understood the doctrine, authority, and responsibility of the church? Remember, we are trying to see the big picture, and if one of the parts is missing or flawed, it affects the whole picture.

- Maybe Satan, the deceiver, has in a major way blinded, distorted, and lessened our understanding of the church in order to divide and immobilize us.

To win a battle, to fulfill a vision, or to carry out any great endeavor will require order, structure, and government. So if the enemy can promote fear and wrong ideas about the church and its authority, then he can make us ineffective.

As we are going to see, church is not a Sunday meeting. It is a governing body that has been given both authority and responsibility to fulfill God's kingdom business, which is certainly something Satan will oppose.

The thoughts that follow are introductory and designed to stimulate discussion. The question is, have we missed seeing something of what

God intends for the church, and is God, through some of the disappointments and conflicts facing us in our various groups trying to get us to climb above the cloud and take a fresh look at this doctrine?

A U-boat has a connection to the admirals in the war room. It has a captain and officers with specific protocols and duties. Without this authority structure and accountability, it would be doomed to ineffectiveness in the battle. So it is with us.

Seven Aspects of Church Structure and Government

I. The church has brotherhood, a body, and equality

The Old Testament people requested a king and a governing system like that of the nations around them. This was never God's desire. He said if they were to have a king, he was not to be richer than anyone else, not to have more horses for going to war, and not to have more wives. In short, he was to be an equal, a brother (Deuteronomy 17:14-20). Despite this command, the people modeled their government according to the nations around them. Their rulers became rich and powerful, lording over the people.

The new wine of the Gospel demands a new wineskin—a relational, brotherly wineskin (Mark 2:22). The government of the Gentiles in which men "exercise authority" over others is "not to be so among you: but whosoever will be great among you, let him be your minister [your servant or better, your slave]" (Matthew 20:25-28; 23:8-12; John 13:13-17; and compare Ephesians 5:3).

The essential ruling dynamic of the church, then, is relational and not institutional, business-minded, or political. We are a family, not bosses and employees, not teachers with a class of students. There will be teachers. There will be leaders. But they must always be brothers and are not to have a title or position that sets them apart from the family. How often we fail, even unconsciously, in this brotherly approach to leadership. We need to pray for a spirit of great humility and brotherly affection to surround all of our relationships in the church. The new wine is contained in a living, relational body, not a temple with services or an organization with programs and hierarchy.

One of the strengths of many Anabaptist-type churches is that they take seriously their *family responsibility* to those who are members. They fix each other's roofs, have barn-raisings, rebuild after a fire, and cover each other's medical expenses. Their young ladies serve as household helpers and as teachers, and their young men volunteer their early work years to help others. They make meals for the sick and for new moms, and care for widows, the elderly, and orphans. Many of these responsibilities have, in the past, been the concern of the family, the church brotherhood, or the community, but today they have largely been taken over by government and insurance programs. This takeover actually robs the church of one valuable form of sharing love as a brotherhood and of learning to trust God in time of need. So one aspect of brotherhood is *taking family responsibility for one another in practical ways.*

Another aspect of brotherhood is what in the past fifty years has been called *body life.* Here we can learn from some of our evangelical brothers and sisters who have emphasized the importance of prayer circles, confessing our needs one to another—not just to a priest—and praying for one another. (Note: This is not just praying for Africa or Aunt Susie, but for one another, right in the group, in the sister's meeting, youth meeting, or men's meeting.) The belief simply is that the members of the body have the gifts of the Spirit needed to minister healing, encouragement, counsel, and correction to other needy members. So brotherhood involves *taking family responsibility to offer spiritual care to one another* in an environment that enables each to minister and receive. Thus, we first see that the church is a relational brotherhood or body in which the members all are equal and each cares for the others in practical and spiritual ways.

II. The church has members with differing roles and gifts in the body (1 Corinthians 12, 14; Ephesians 4:8-16; Romans 12:5-8; 1 Peter 4:10-11)

For the body to work properly, every member needs to be employed doing his part. Some will have a larger part and some a smaller part. Some have more maturity, while others are just starting out. Some are older and others younger. Some have recognized callings as elders, deacons, or ministering widows (1 Timothy 5), but all are needed. It is understood that the giftings of the body come from the Spirit, so no one can take the credit. Furthermore, the youngest or simplest member may be the one the Spirit uses or speaks through, for gifts are not signs of maturity, but of availability. They are based on God's choice and operate according to the measure of the individual's faith.

III. The church has the God-given gift of leaders to the body (1 Corinthians 12:28-29; Romans 12:8; Ephesians 4:11; 1 Timothy 3; Titus 1)

Leaders are one of the gifts God has given to the body. They are an integral part of the working of the body. Not much happens in the world without leaders to set direction, dream, inspire others, organize, and mobilize people to action. Having said that, let us remember that leaders are first equal and servants to the body. In one sense, they are less important than others, for if the church had only leaders, nothing would get done.

A brother that once gave oversight to our congregation stated that the effective church needs both strong leadership and strong brotherhood. Having one without the other leads to a weaker church.

Consider as an example an Amish barn-raising. Two hundred men are needed to work in unity to get the job done in a day, but one man and some foremen plan and organize the details. If all two hundred had needed to agree on the best way to do the work, they might never have started. If they all were the leader, they probably would never finish.

Leaders come in many forms (Ephesians 4:11-13):

- **Apostles** serve the larger church body by advancing the work of the kingdom to new frontiers, new towns, and new ministries. They are sent to pioneer, inspire, oversee, unite churches, and call the whole church to take new territory.

- **Prophets** see what God wants and call the church to deal with sin and become what God intends.

- **Pastors** shepherd, nurture, and feed the local flock, watching over its needs, and guarding it against wolves.

- **Teachers** specialize in instructing and training the small class, the local congregation, or the larger church . They should pass on not their own ideas but a common deposit of faith (2 Timothy 2:2).

- **Evangelists** are particularly gifted and set apart to proclaim the Gospel, and to inspire and equip the church to fulfill its role in reaching the lost.

The Bible speaks of **ordaining** (recognizing/setting apart) some proven, mature men as elders/ministers to form a team to take responsibility for watching over the direction and teaching of the church. Some of these ordained men will function more as teaching-elders. Some function as the pastor-elders and some are ruling-elders [decision makers/direction setters/bishops/overseers] (1 Timothy 5:17; 3:4-5; Romans 12:8; Hebrews 13:7, 17, 24).

- Elders/ministers, then, *function in the context or environment of a relational brotherhood.* That means their leadership is to have a family atmosphere. They are not above the church family; they are part of it. In fact, it is the church family that assembles, prays, nominates, interviews, and finally ordains elders (ministers) to serve and lead. In a brotherhood-centered church or fellowship of churches, all the members have chosen and committed themselves to an established direction. Their ministers have been ordained to instruct and guide the brotherhood in the values, standards, and direction that the *assembly has already agreed to follow.* So leadership is always connected to the assembly. On the other hand, in the minister-centered church, the direction, values, and expectations are established and changed by the minister(s). The people merely decide if they want to be part of the ministers' church. There is no responsible brotherhood assembly.

- Elders are Spirit-anointed, proven men called and set apart by the local church to serve it and to *equip and strengthen the whole church to get its job done.*

- Elders may *function in many different ways* according to their giftings and the needs (apostle, pastor, prophet, teacher, evangelist, administrator, bishop, etc.).

- There should always be a *plurality* of these men serving in a local church because many different gifts and viewpoints are needed to create a balanced leadership team that can build the whole body. This team of seasoned men models the unity and life expected of the whole body. Especially in small or new works this plurality would include overseers or ministers from other congregations.

- Something to bear in mind is that this word *elder* and the list of qualifications for ministers (1 Timothy 3:4-6) indicate that the elders/ministers are more *elderly, experienced, and proven in life,* especially in family life. (Also note this same inference for those who serve as deacons 1 Timothy 3:12.) Some established, conservative groups effectively include junior ministers in an in-training role together with men in their forties, sixties, and eighties. Revival-type groups with little structure often lack these older men and thus put undue pressure on men with young families and no mentors. Seeking an ongoing relationship with some mature elders should be made a prayerful priority.

- These men in leadership should be *freed up* and supported by the people in proportion to the amount and nature of the work they have been called to do (1 Timothy 5:17-18; Luke 10:7). The congregation, according to its size and ability, is to pray for and support a supply of shepherds for the flock and of laborers for the harvest field (Matthew 9:36-38).

• The calling and ordaining of elders is a *serious business,* and they are to meet scriptural qualifications (1 Timothy 3). They must be prepared to give themselves to the work. It is not to be merely a hobby or a side job for their spare time, but a vocation given by God and His people. When they are asked, "What is your line of work?" their response is, "I am a minister of the Gospel of Jesus Christ, and on the side I support myself as a carpenter." The energy, time, and resources that were once invested in learning carpentry, better farming skills, or building a business are now invested in actively learning and giving oneself to a whole new calling.

• Elders *are to rule.* That literally means to stand out front and lead. They are to teach, oversee, and protect. If they are to effectively do so, they must be honored and obeyed, with the recognition that what they have to say will not always be popular or even right; they will make mistakes (1 Timothy 5:17; Hebrews 13:7, 17).

• Elders and teachers *come under a stricter judgment* and will give account to God for their role as watchmen, direction-setters, teachers, and pastors of God's flock (James 3:1; Hebrews 13:17; 1 Peter 5:2-4; Ezekiel 33:1-6; Jeremiah 23; Matthew 23).

• To bring a complaint or accusation against an elder is serious business and should be undertaken only with two or three witnesses. If sin is found in the elder(s), it is not to be dealt with privately but brought before the whole church for judgment. This legislation both *protects* the elders against the complaining that makes their job more grievous and makes the elders more *accountable* for their failures if wrong is found in them by the assembly (1 Timothy 5:19-22).

One other leadership role in the church is that of **deacons** (Acts 6; 1 Timothy 3; Titus 1).

• In Acts 6, **deacons**, or servers, *take care of practical and relational needs and problems* in the congregation of God's people (6:1) so that the elders *are freed to give themselves to the Word and to prayer*. Take note in what was just said about what the deacons are called to do (6:3) and what the elders are to be freed for (6:2, 4). Deacons, then, are more than money handlers and junior preachers. They are men of wisdom, practicality, and administration. They are first to be tested and proven and then set apart for this responsibility as problem solvers and practical organizers in the church family. A friend of mine told me that in his younger years problems of all kinds usually were dealt with by the deacons so that the ministers were free to preach, unhindered by loads of problems or blame for how they were handled. As time went on, the ministers got more involved in handling problems, and he felt that in the long run, the church and her ministers suffered as a result. We would do well to consider the testimony of the New Testament church that appointed Spirit-filled men (Acts 6) to handle the potentially damaging relational and economic problems that arose amongst them.

Leadership is not a position. It is a function of service in the body and to the kingdom. In a large construction project, different men lead at different times depending on the various stages of the work. Likewise, in the church, leadership is to be determined by the needs at hand and the leading of the Spirit. In the New Testament era, the apostles each had unique ways in which they were gifted and functioned best, but they were not threatened or in competition with each other.

It is very important to remember that all of these leaders are just members of the body who have been given a specific function by God. They are to coach, equip, and help the body to grow, to operate harmoniously, and to get the job done. They are not outside the body, nor are they above it. They are brothers with needs like everyone else. Their job may sound appealing, but it is not easy, and it comes with a warning: "My brethren, be not many masters, knowing that we shall receive the greater condemnation" (James 3:1).

Let's review:

So far in this chapter we have seen that in structure:

    I. The church is a relational brotherhood or body of equals.

    II. Members each have been given differing gifts and roles.

    III. Leadership is one of these many gifts.

IV. The church (ecclesia) is to be ordered and governed

If we go back to our previous illustration depicting the government of a country or a town (refer to the end of Pillar 8 on page 116), we can learn some things about this point. We know that without order, our countries and towns would be in chaos. Government provides rule and order in several ways. I will list them here, then come back and apply them to the church later:

1. Government **sets moral laws** (such as "Don't Murder") and punishments for violators (death or prison).

2. Government **sets laws of order** to bring harmony (obey speed limits, drive on the right side, don't text while driving, etc.), and breaking these may get you a warning or a fine. They are not moral laws, but they do help all of life work better.

3. Government **seeks to organize things to improve its people's way of living** (well planned roads, new parks, etc). Every government has different ideas as to what good improvements actually are.

4. Government *seeks to protect* the land and property of its citizens.

5. Government *meets, or assembles together regularly* to make laws and decisions and to carry out actions that benefit the country and bring peace and order. They need to study and research to

find the best way to do this. Then they need to present it and discuss it in the legislative assembly.

Now, let's return to the church brotherhood. This idea of the legislative assembly is the essential meaning of the term *ecclesia* in the Greek language used in the original writing of the New Testament. In English this word is translated as church. It literally means *called out ones*—called out from everyday life to do the political business of a city or country. For us as Christians, it means called out of the world and gathered to hear God and do His kingdom business.

In the Old Testament Jewish world, the elders *assembled* at the gate of the city to discuss things, to make decisions, and to judge the people. Israel often was called to assemble to hear something God or the king had to say. In the Greek world, the citizens of a city *assembled* to discuss business, appoint leaders, and make decisions. Likewise, an assembly, an *ecclesia*, a church, is a gathering out of citizens to study, to discuss, to make decisions, to instruct, to appoint leaders, to assign responsibilities, and to direct the life of the whole people.

Those who can officially take part in the interaction of this assembly are the responsible, committed citizens (the members).

This Brotherhood Assembly Has Governmental Order

1. Christ is the Head.

2. Man is under, subject to, Him.

3. Woman is under, subject to, man.

Man is responsible. He is called to speak and lead *in the assembly*, and the woman is to remain quiet and not to lead men. As a reminder of this and as a symbol of her willing submission to God's order, the woman is to cover her head. When covered and under the authority of the man, she has authority to pray and prophesy, but in the assembly gathered for instruction, study, and decision making, she is to remain quiet and allow

God to work through the brothers (1 Corinthians 11; 1 Corinthians 14:33-40; 1 Timothy 2:8-15; 1 Timothy 3; 1 Peter 3:1-7).

Much confusion, chaos, and destruction have come to our society, our homes, and our marriages because of the rejection and reversal of God's headship order. It is imperative that we as God's prophetic people seek to discern and chart a path back to the point in the road where we departed from God's order. To paddle against the stream of our society and of most of the Christian world will be difficult work and will receive much opposition, but there is no other way to reverse the curse and find true liberation in obedience to God's unchanging instructions.

This Brotherhood Assembly Has Interaction

Many *assemblies* or church services today are characterized by one-way communication, directed from the pulpit to the pew. There is little study, interaction, seeking the mind of God, or decision making. These may take place later in a council, monthly brotherhood meeting, or an annual members meeting, but this does not appear to be faithful to the original nature of the regular assembly. The original New Testament assembly seemed to be much more interactive. It was assumed that all would be involved and that those speaking would sit down when some-one else had something to say (1 Corinthians 14). In fact, it seems the inter-involvement was so great that it was disorderly and Paul wrote 1 Corinthians 12 and 14 to teach principles of *order*.

Also, unlike today's service, the word *assembly* originally indicated a body gathered to discuss the issues of the day and to determine the proper direction and decisions. It was the community meeting to hear Jesus, the Head, speaking to the members and giving them His directions. This was to be no once-in-a-while event. The church had two kinds of meetings: those for hearing from God and applying it to life (i.e., for governing and instruction) and those for worship and the Lord's table.

This Brotherhood Assembly Has the Responsibility to Govern in His Name

Jesus said that wherever two or three gather in His Name, there He is present, there is the church. To these believers gathered in His Name (i.e., in His authority, under His signature), He gives the governing keys of the kingdom of heaven as well as the right and serious responsibility to discern, to act, to bind, and to loose, not in their own names, but in His Name. The "two or three" or more who are gathered (the New Testament Greek word here is *synagogued*) are to agree together as to God's desire (agree is the Greek word *symphony*). This means that both *horizontal* discussion, evaluation, and vital *vertical* communication must take place. The end result is to be a symphony of agreement, followed by authoritative action.

This is no light matter. It seems very significant that *the only statements of Jesus about the church* have to do with this responsibility to first discern and then to act under His authority to bind and loose (stop and command), in order that His kingdom business on earth is accomplished in His absence (Matthew 16:18-19; 18:15-20).

In light of what I have outlined, I want to impress upon you the seriousness of this *governing responsibility* given to the brothers. Recently, a godly, surrendered minister of the Gospel told me something shocking. He said that based on what he has experienced, he would not entrust decisions about his life and direction to a brotherhood. He would not trust the brotherhood to set values that would be solid enough to guide his family. Why would a man who is under authority say such a thing? As a parable and to teach a lesson, let's get the brotherhood involved in a problem on the job site:

> A young brother in our church opens a small engine repair shop and one day spends a couple of hours trying to get a clutch out of a snowmobile. Let's imagine that he decides to consult the brotherhood for some input and agrees to follow their instructions for solving the problem. Would we be of much use to him? Off the

top of our heads we could give him all kinds of advice: use a crow bar; guard your attitude; and hire reliable help. We could tell him he shouldn't be working on snowmobiles anyhow, and so on. We could finally vote that he should give the customer his bill with apologies and then humbly find another line of work.

What is the problem with all of that instruction? If you were that young mechanic wanting help from your brothers, would you feel encouraged with the help of the brotherhood? If you were the snowmobile owner, would you be impressed with the brothers' wisdom? What if this scenario repeated itself every time a problem or a major business decision needed to be made?

Let's go back and apply this parable to God's kingdom business. What if the brotherhood is asked to make a decision about direction on the mission field, suitable music for a choral group, starting an orphanage, selecting who should preach or lead worship, painting the church kitchen, doing summer evangelism, or discipling the youth? Suppose the brotherhood is asked to discuss and set direction concerning biblical economics in God's kingdom, insurance, modesty, Internet protection, electronic gadgets, courtship, or supervision of children after church services.

How will we approach these situations posing a problem to solve, a vision to be established, or a decision to be made? Will we also do it off of the top of our heads? A few vital ingredients are needed if a godly and helpful decision is to be made:

1. The *ecclesia* must have a *good connection with the Head,* Jesus Christ, through a life of serious prayer, Bible study and listening to God—**Communion**.

2. *Good communication with those most involved* in the area of concern or ministry is essential—**Community**.

3. *All the facts and information need to be gathered and laid out on the table:* facts about the situation and facts from the Bible—the big picture, as well as detailed study of relevant verses and biblical

examples of similar situations. (Some of this may be delegated to two or three for research)—**Commitment**.

4. *Prayer must be focused on all that is involved*, accompanied by *waiting* until there is a sense that God's will is known (e.g. Hezekiah in 2 Kings 19:14ff)—**Communication**.

5. Together the assembly must *make the decision* and follow through with appropriate action—**Church** (Ecclesia).

Can you see how serious this kingdom business is? Can you see the *commitment of time* and *careful thought* that is needed? Can you, based on your brotherhood experience, see why the brother I mentioned earlier might have a reason to feel he could not trust his life and direction to the decisions of the average brotherhood? Can you see how lighthearted we as ministers, brotherhoods, and committees sometimes are about God's work? On the other hand, can you see the united authority and power that could be the result if we took *being the church* seriously? It's time to wake up and change some of our expectations about godly decision making. I have seen too many meetings and decisions where there was no earnest prayer, no searching of the Scriptures, no open communication with the people most involved, no waiting on God for a united answer, and no effective follow-up and action. (The five steps listed above will help any group make decisions more responsibly. Why not write them down in the book you use at your ministers meeting, brothers meeting, or committee meeting?)

The point I am trying to make is that the church as a whole has been given a job and the authority to carry it out. The church as a whole community has been called to live out godly values, and thus be a prophetic witness to the surrounding culture. The church as a body is to disciple and, as needed, discipline the wayward.

All of this is spiritual work in which we must be united. The exact mechanics of how each group does this may vary, but it is important that we accept and define our corporate responsibility and get to the work.

Again, I am not suggesting that every decision must go through the brotherhood. That would be hopelessly boring and inefficient, and would set aside the responsibility of leadership and of each individual's giftedness. In a great symphony, each part is important, and each instrumentalist needs to know what he is doing. But if the musicians expect people to pay to listen, they must all be in unity and committed to the same task.

By the way, it took only two men—the right two men—to solve the problem with the snowmobile's clutch. The shop door opened and in walked an experienced mechanic looking for work. The two men started chatting about the project in the back and five minutes later the clutch was out. The right man walked through the door—the one who could actually be a help—and guess what? He was hired.

Another quick review:

(Then we will dig deeper into the nature of brotherhood responsibility.)

We have been saying that:

IV. **The church (ecclesia) is to be *ordered* and *governed***

- There is a governmental headship order to submit to.
- There is to be interaction and involvement from all the members.
- There is serious responsibility to govern in Jesus' name.

So, what of this responsibility to assemble to govern? What does it involve? I suggest that we use the tasks of a country or town government mentioned earlier as an outline (see page 132).

Outline for a Brotherhood Government

1. The brotherhood *submits to the moral and ethical behavioral laws and commands set by God.* God has told us specific things we are not to do and specific things we are to do. These are rules He has already laid down for all people of all times.

The brotherhood does not judge those outside the church—that is God's job—but it does judge those within, those who are committed members, for judgment must begin within the house of God (1 Corinthians 5-6). Jesus said that a little leaven leavens the whole lump, so purge out the leaven of wickedness *before* it has a chance to ruin the whole loaf (Matthew 18; 1 Corinthians 5:7, 13).

God lays out the normative way that moral sins and other offenses are to be addressed and resolved (1 Corinthians 6:1-4). They are to be dealt with regularly and quickly, first by the concerned individual approaching the wayward member, and then if this fails, by one or two other godly, and preferably impartial, people enlisted to help resolve and be witnesses.

Finally, if need be, the offender is to be brought before the church (assembly) so that they can discern what is right, and then with united agreement either bind or loose (Matthew 18:15-22). If the wayward member will not hear the appeals of the assembly, he or she is to be released from membership in the church family and be treated as a heathen or worldly person. Those with moral sin are to be "put away from among yourselves" (from your group) and not "kept company with" (1 Corinthians 5:9, 11, 13).

In all of this, remember that the attitude is to be a brotherly longing for restoration and not one of punishment. Note that the words of Jesus immediately following the discussion on discipline in Matthew 18 have to do with the importance of being willing to forgive (verses 21-35). Also see 2 Corinthians 2:8-11 on the imperative of forgiving and of reaffirming love to the repentant. All those involved must consider themselves and first judge themselves, knowing that in the way they judge they will be judged (Galatians 6:1; Matthew 7:1-5). It therefore seems there are two possible biblical choices when I face difficulties with a brother or sister:

- I can practice loving forbearance, patience, and prayer.

—or—

- I can approach them in love as I would with a fellow family member.

If I fail to practice one of these two scriptural options, I likely will fall into a trap of sin *myself* in one of two unbiblical ways:

- I will speak evil of my brother instead of speaking to him (Ephesians 4:31; James 4:11; 5:9; Matthew 7:1-5; Romans 2:1; 12:14-21).

—or—

- I will build up a mountain of bitterness, envy, and strife, which will consume me and maybe defile many others (e.g. Saul in 1 Samuel 18:7-12; Psalm 119:165; Matthew 24:10; 1 John 2:9-11).

Therefore, the brotherhood is responsible to fulfill the governmental duties of teaching and also upholding God's moral laws. But this is to be done in the context of a natural, consistent, brotherly, caring, relational family environment (not a courtroom atmosphere). This sobering and serious business must not be avoided, or it will be difficult to fix later.

2. The brotherhood assembly also has the right to study, discuss, and discern how to *legislate things that bring* **order**, harmony, and a united witness in the everyday life of the community of God's people.

The laws in this case are not moral. They are to help the body have *order*. They relate to schedule, etiquette, and timeliness; to applications that further modesty, simplicity, meeting needs, common practices, music, raising children, courtship standards, and all the practical details for which we are to be of "one mind" in order to support one another and have a corporate community culture and witness (Philippians 1:27; 2:2; 1 Corinthians 1:10; Romans 15:5-6).

These laws allow more room for growth, grace for newcomers, consideration of exceptions, and the need for periodic reviewing, but the goal is *order* and a united witness. Therefore, anything leading to disorder, division, or individualism needs to be instructed, corrected, and, if need be, disciplined because of disregard for the appeal of the brothers and the need for unity.

Some may ask whether the church has a right to give direction in practical things not clearly spelled out in the Bible. The common concern is with becoming legalistic, *but this fear of legalism actually keeps us from discussing and seeking God's will in heaven concerning practical life here on earth.* As a result, we allow worldliness to grow and we say nothing. Many times the charge of legalism is a cloak to cover our desire to go our own way (to disobey), to be a little less different than the world, or to have things a little easier.

Another objection to brotherly involvement from the church community is that "Individuals and families need to be given the freedom to follow their own consciences." Many have been victims of an ugly authoritarianism forced on the group by its leaders. In such cases, however, the action was not a collective brotherhood agreement. It was something from outside or from above the brotherhood imposed on it. Because the brotherhood did not own these enforced convictions, the result had the potential to produce bitterness, resistance, and evil speaking against the leaders.

The alternative to this is the regular work of asking questions and studying the Scriptures, the doctrine, and the world around us, and then together applying the Word of God to our lives. As we saw earlier in the snowmobile example, this takes time and serious commitment, but it is essential work for the whole brotherhood if they are to be of one mind.

Someone has suggested that the men should be in some way doing this every Sunday in a men's doctrine class. This seems more in line with the early church and would certainly help men to think and be raised up as leaders. Someone else has suggested retreats every five or ten years, at which the beliefs, practices, and direction of the church are reviewed, reevaluated, and renewed. (Between retreats they are obeyed.)

I am suggesting that the church does have the right and responsibility to make brotherly agreements and seek to establish a godly culture in our day. I am suggesting that *this general direction setting is the job of the brotherhood (or better yet, of a group of brotherhoods) and not just the function of individuals or families.*

In other words, the collective church and her leaders act to instruct, direct, and present a godly pattern of life to families and individuals. It is not individuals or families each doing what is right in their own eyes and seeking to influence the church. That is not unity or community. It is a group of individualists who gather for their mutual convenience and not for mutual accountability and brotherhood.

Again, I share from my background. In our former setting, it was an unwritten rule that each home had its own ways and problems, and generally the pastor and church were not expected to meddle into them. If the preaching got too practical, the preacher was in trouble. He could preach on drunkenness or maybe immodesty, but he had no brotherhood assembly to come to an agreement, follow through, and deal with those who drank alcohol or were immodest. The pastor could do little alone and if he tried to deal with problems the church would shrink or he would be replaced. He could preach against the evils of fornication, but he could only love those who fell into it. He could not gather the fathers or young people and agree to some standards as a church for godly courtship and less flirtatious dress. Such things were the family's domain, and besides, it was accepted that most people would fall into some failure in these areas.

Consequently, in the average church there might be only one or two families seeking to go against the flow and set a godly pattern. But they were surrounded by a majority in the church who were unconcerned and actually mocked those who had standards for dating, decided to be keepers at home, eliminated television, or supervised their children's play. Thus the church environment often was unsupportive and even hostile, the very opposite of what a church should be.

Because of this very dilemma, many people are traveling and even moving across the country seeking like-minded fellowship. But what does it take to establish and maintain this kind of godly and supportive environment in which to raise and disciple our families? It doesn't just happen. Someone has to do some heavenly thinking, direction setting, and actual submitting. Unfortunately, these seekers who have stood alone against ungodly worldly directions in former churches, often are unwilling or unable to submit in small things to the new brotherhood they have found. They are used to setting their own direction and have a hard time submitting to the brotherhood direction they so desperately sought to find.

The critical question is *who sets the direction*? Who determines the beliefs and practices—the gathered church or each individual? Of this you can be sure: *someone will set the direction.* The question again is, *who?* Lines of acceptable practice will be drawn somewhere—but how low will we allow them to be drawn? If we brothers don't draw general lines regarding television, Internet, fashion, sports, foolishness, and the like, someone else will. It may be our youth, the sisters, or a new struggling family that actually needs discipleship and direction. Congregations always will have both people who are more conservative and those who are more liberal. There will be new or struggling believers and also mature, established ones. But still the question is, do we go down low to the level of the less discerning members in order to keep them and preserve unity? Do we let them set the standard, or do we seek patiently to set a vision and make disciples? Do we seek to survive alone as individuals swimming against the current of society, or do we accept the serious responsibility of establishing like-minded fellowships and groups of fellowships that can be communities of light and encouragement?

Many have come from families where a dad and mom dared to stand alone and set a different and godly direction, and it bore fruit. But what will it take to have *a whole church family* that *together* takes a like-minded stand in that same way? It should not be that individual families need to stand alone within our churches, for it is the church itself that has been called to stand alone against the surrounding darkness. Let us rise to the task.

Following are some Scriptures indicating that the church as a new people group has the right to establish general standards in practical and cultural areas and to pass them to other churches:

- The Thessalonians became "*followers* of the churches in Judea" (1 Thessalonians 2:14).

- They *followed* Paul and his traditions (1 Thessalonians 1:6-7; 4:1-2; 2:14; 2 Thessalonians 2:15; 3:7).

- They, in turn, became *patterns* to new believers in Macedonia and Achaia (1 Thessalonians 1:7).

- Paul urges the Philippians to *follow* the practical example of his conduct and live just as if he were actually there (Philippians 1:27; 2:2, 12; 3:16-18; 4:9).

- Paul commends the Corinthians for *following* him and remembering his ways which he taught "in every church." He also instructs them about headship and head coverings, things that he says are the "*practice* in all the churches." Later he instructs them about the *common order* in the services, which is to establish "peace in all the churches" (1 Corinthians 4:15-17; 7:17; 11:1, 2, 16; 14:33, 37).

- Similar passages can be found in 1 Timothy 3:15; 4:11-12; 2 Timothy 3:10, 14; Titus 2:7.

These Scriptures indicate that the entire early church had many practices in common. In practical things and church life, they followed the example of Paul and of other mature churches. They did not just do what they as individuals thought was right.

On the other hand, it also is clear that they had some differences in how they did things (Revelation 2-3). In the "how-tos" of life, England governs itself differently than Canada or Ghana. Likewise, we need not impose our exact *order* on to other local churches. The important thing is that we need to see ourselves as a people governed as a brotherhood in such a way that there is *order* and a beautiful united witness.

The governments of our countries and towns additionally perform other jobs:

3. They *plan and carry out programs that improve life and benefit the community.*

4. They *protect* the country from evil.

5. They are committed to *meet, or assemble, together regularly.*

These also are normal functions of the brotherhood and those it appoints to lead out in these areas. Perhaps you struggle with this idea of church government, but take note, every group *will* govern itself somehow. This can be done in many ways—good and bad—so it is important that we *think* seriously about this subject and *seek to be clear* about what our beliefs, practices, responsibilities, and governing structures are. If not, the result will be confusion, disorder, and more opportunity for evil speaking, disunity, and failure. The biblical pattern that Paul lays out in 1 Corinthians embraces both the freedom of the *Spirit* and also *order*. These two things do not fight against each other but rather complement each other and together express the church in all its intended beauty.

Summing up what we have seen so far in this chapter...

It is important that we recognize the biblical framework of the governing of the assembly as follows:

I.   The church is a *relational* and equal brotherhood.

II. In the church, each member is committed to be an active part of the life and governing process, and to work according to his or her specific *gifts* and roles.

III. In the church, mature *leadership* is ordained to help the brotherhood fulfill its goals.

IV. In the church, there needs to be *order* and *government*. The brothers are responsible to uphold the purity and order of the church community and to advance the work of the kingdom. They have the right and obligation to make general brotherhood agreements and decisions that help maintain order and one-minded direction.

Please note: The question we have been considering with this pillar is this: Do we all govern our spiritual lives individually or is there an authoritative place for a brotherhood or fellowship of churches and the appointed leaders to govern the lives and direction of its members? The primary issue I am raising is not whether leadership is by brotherhood or by elders/ministers. The answer to that, I believe, is that leadership is by both, though different groups will work out the details in different ways.

My thesis here is that the modern world has deified man and given authority to the individual. This *transference of authority* to the individual has greatly affected the church, including those of us in Radical Believers' Churches, and it has clouded and distorted our picture of God's kingdom people and purposes. *If we are to bring together the pieces of the puzzle that form the big picture of God's design, then it is essential that we recognize and reaffirm the governing authority and responsibility of the church—the ecclesia.*

We now address the fifth major point regarding the church as it assembles.

V. The church (ecclesia) is a worshiping community

The church seeks to instruct and build up the body so that they in life, word, praise, prayer, and song can worship Jesus Christ. God's people gather regularly to do this. They also come together for other important acts of worship that have been commanded by Christ.

Water Baptism—All Christians are to have a clear believer's baptism that testifies to the inner reality of the new birth, and the passing from darkness to light. In this baptism they publicly declare that they have been buried with Christ and raised to the newness of His life (Matthew 28:19; Romans 6:1-5; 1Peter 3:21).

The Lord's Supper—This meal is to be observed regularly by baptized believers who are examined and walking clear before God and man. Any hindrances are to be quickly resolved by the individual or brotherhood (1 Corinthians 11:27-32). In partaking of the Lord's Supper, we are remembering the Lord's death (1 Corinthians 11:24) giving thanks for it (1 Corinthians 11:24a), and declaring that He died for us (1 Corinthians 11:26). It is clear in 1 Corinthians 11 that this is a community meal that witnesses both to what the Lord has done for us and also to the unity we have as a people because of what He has done. The belief in the communal nature of this meal places restrictions on who can participate. This is based on the belief that we must "discern the body" (1 Corinthians 11:29-33) before we eat, in other words, we must be speaking into one another's lives, dealing with hindrances and sin, and seeking the restoration and unity of the body so that our eating is a testimony of our oneness in Christ. Perhaps we need to give more serious thought to this serious responsibility and privilege.

Foot Washing—This literal use of the basin and towel was commanded by the Lord as a continual reminder of His servant nature. It also is a reminder that our attitude in the brotherhood must always be that of serving and putting others first. Without this, brotherhood will not work (John 13:1-17).

These acts of obedience and worship are important, but a command above them all, without which everything we have said will fail, is the one given by Jesus when He said: "A new commandment I give unto you, that ye love one another; as I have loved you, that ye also love one another; by this shall all men know that ye are my disciples, if ye have love one to another" (John 13:34-35). Services, standards, brotherly agreements, gifts, and leadership all are important, but the oil that lubricates all of these and makes them work is showing patience, forbearance, forgiveness, and grace to one another. We need faith, hope, and love for our brothers and sisters (1 Corinthians 13). All of this is brotherhood. Who will find it? Will you?

Another word needs to be considered in our original statement on the church. That word is *members*.

VI. The church has members

Without a commitment of like-minded people voluntarily banding together in love for the common good, there will be no clear peoplehood, no distinct, united community, and no real way to disciple, to make decisions, or to discipline. The interaction, government, brotherhood agreements, and accountability of a local brotherhood will not work unless people choose and commit themselves to be part of it. The leaders and brothers must commit time for prayer, communal study of the Word, open discussion and ministry.

The kind of local church described here is not the only way to order the church. Many dynamic churches have operated with other patterns. Our desire has been to consider the possibility of a biblical model for the church in which a *strong, committed brotherhood* becomes a base for *visionary leadership* and for the *effective advance of God's kingdom business*. To put it another way,

> Strong Brotherhood
> + Strong Leadership (both ordained and lay leadership)
> _____
> = A Strong Church (that gets the job done)

The church is not just a gathering for services, sermons, or programs. It is not just an invisible, universal church. It is a visible, practical, local expression of the life of heaven, and for that it needs real, visible, committed people. May God give you the reality of this kind of brotherhood to pass on to the next generation. So many people complain about their churches, but why do we not instead commit ourselves to the beautiful actions that God says will cause the church to work?

We have been looking at various aspects of the life of the church as it assembles. Our declarative statement at the onset of Pillar 9 says:

> **We believe the church (the *ecclesia*)**
>
> **is a worshiping community** (V),
>
> **ordered and governed** (IV)
>
> **as a brotherhood or body** (II and III)
>
> **of equal** (I) **members** (VI),
>
> **under the headship of Jesus Christ** (VII).

Man has a vital part in God's order of things. But we must remember this last point. It is Christ who is the Head.

VII. The church submits to Christ as the Head

The whole action of the assembled and, later, scattered church in worship, ministry, mission, and government is dependent on the Headship of Christ. It is His will that we desire to see worked out on earth as it is planned in heaven. It is He who will "do exceedingly abundantly above all we could ask or think according to the power [His power] that worketh in us" (Ephesians 3:20).

Let's consider some examples of

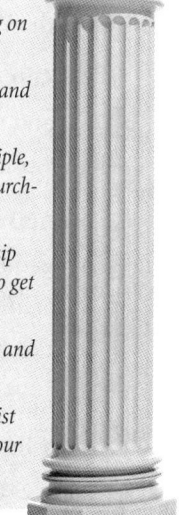

Blessings
of Embracing Pillar 9:

Benefits of the working ecclesia:

- *The brotherhood has clear agreements.*

- *We are committed to make practical decisions together.*

- *We experience the joy of hearing God, making applications, and acting on them together.*

- *We have clarity to bind and loose.*

- *We can confidently disciple, discipline, and plant churches.*

- *Ministers are free to equip and enable the church to get the job done.*

- *We experience true love and brotherhood.*

- *We truly know that Christ the Head is working in our midst.*

Christ, present in and at work in and through the gathered believers in the book of Acts (the history detailing the first years of the church):

- **Acts 1:14-26:** Jesus ascended to heaven and then 120 of the serious believers **assembled** in an upper room and spent the next weeks in continual prayer. What Scripture study, confession, making things right with each other, and calling out to God must have happened in that room! In those days, Peter was given a word of direction and spoke of the need to replace the traitor Judas. *God directed,* and a man named Matthias was chosen.

- **Acts 2:** As the disciples were still **assembled** in one accord in one place, waiting on God, a mighty rushing wind filled the house and those present were filled with the Holy Ghost. All marveled, and again Peter was *given a prophetic word* from the Head of the church. As a result, many souls were added.

- **Acts 4:31-33:** A group **assembled** to pray, and suddenly *the Holy Ghost came and filled them* with power and they spoke the Word of the Lord with boldness. The great multitude of these new believers were more and more united in heart. They all shared what they owned to meet the needs, and powerful ministry resulted, all because God was their active Head.

- **Acts 6:4:** The leaders committed themselves to prayer and study of the Word, *to hear what the Head desired* for the whole body.

- **Acts 13:1-3:** Prophets and teachers **assembled** to worship and fast, and *God told them* to separate Saul and Barnabas for missionary work.

- **Acts 15:** The apostles and elders, and at times the whole congregation, **assembled** to consider some church problems, and again *God spoke* through all the group and then specifically through Peter and James.

- **Acts 19:9-10:** Paul **assembled** believers daily for two years at the school of Tyrannus, and from those gatherings *God led* new disciples all over Asia speaking forth the Word of the Lord Jesus.

Wherever believers *assembled* with Christ as the Head something happened that was seen and that affected the world around them. It can be the same way with us if *we take the time,* as they did, to gather, believing *we can and must hear from Him* concerning His will in heaven. It is then that we can bind and loose, speak, and go forth with His power and authority. This leads us to our next pillar which concerns the job we have been given to do in His place. We have been given a commission, a job to do while we are here.

MEMORY AID

- Pillar 1—COMMUNION—**God exists**—Intimate Relationship
- Pillar 2—COMMUNICATION—**God has spoken**—Hear and Obey
- Pillar 3—COMMUNITY— **Peoplehood**—Prophetic Peoplehood
- Pillar 4—CITIZENSHIP—**The Kingdom of God**—The "Upside Down" Kingdom
- Pillar 5—COMMITMENT—**Discipleship**—Following Christ in Life
- Pillar 6—CONVERSION—**The New Birth**—Christ the Door to Life
- Pillar 7—CONFESSION—**Faith**—Faith is the Key
- Pillar 8—CROSS-BEARING—**Humility**—Dying Daily
- Pillar 9—CHURCH—**Ecclesia**—The Relational Governing Structure and Order of God's Distinct New Society
- Pillar 10—COMMISSION—**Missions**—The Church's Task

Seeds of the Faith—Pillar 10

The faith stands as mighty pillars, solid and unchanging. It rises as glorious mountain peaks, but it began its work in me as little seeds.

As a nine-year-old boy I stood listening to my Dad preach at the monument in Old Chitambo where the heart of David Livingstone was buried. I loved Africa, but I never dreamed of being a missionary. Besides, I was a quiet, withdrawn boy, at least until I had my accident. Then many things changed. I began to talk, to interact, and to pray. Praying can be dangerous business. God can speak to you and give direction to your life. And so it was that the distinct impression came to my wife and me that we were to get involved in ministry in the community surrounding the Bible School that I was to be attending and that I was to go visiting people door-to-door. So it was that during those years we helped start a boys' and girls' club and a community Sunday school, and I went out each week knocking on doors.

At first, the very thought of door-to-door evangelism filled me with terror, but once I began, all that changed, and it became my great joy. I don't know if those years bore much fruit in others, but God did a work in me. He put missions on my heart. Not missions in Africa, but missions right here at home. That seed of missions began to grow as I obeyed and simply went out in Jesus' name. I still wasn't much of a talker. I still didn't know all the Bible said about missions and evangelism, but God had said, "Go," so I went.

Soon after this, two great Scriptures began to shape my thinking and desires. I was gripped by the accounts of Jesus sending out His disciples from town to town with the Gospel of the kingdom. But even more compelling was a story in the Book of Acts of Paul teaching for two years at the school of Tyrannus and of all Asia hearing the Gospel as a result.

I wasn't called to Africa, but I knew that church life was more than singing and listening to sermons. The church was to be a people of mission. That mission began here in our own country, and somehow I wanted to be part of making it happen.

PILLAR 10

Missions

*We believe the church has been left on the earth
to be a visible witness of the life of heaven.
We have been given a commission to take the
message of the Gospel (good news) of Jesus and
His kingdom into all the world.*

In a town close to where I live, there is an old, historic hotel. One of its brick walls collapsed in a storm recently, and the town council has ordered the owner to demolish the whole structure. When a wall is missing, everyone knows it. The situation is dangerous, and immediate action must be taken.

We now are considering a pillar of the faith which must not be missing or the whole structure will be in danger. The church has been given a mission, a commission. There is a job to be done on this earth. The God of heaven *sent His Son to begin that job,* and then *to pass on the responsibility to others, to us.* That job has been given to the church, His working body here on earth.

We Inherit His Job

This job—**missions**—is God's idea. He started it. He was the first sender; He sent His Son. His Son left His comfort zone to come to us. The first words of this missionary Jesus to His first apprentices were, "Follow me, and I will make you fishers of men" (Matthew 4:19). That is, "Follow me and *you can inherit my job,* my business; you can preach repentance and the gospel of the kingdom" (Matthew 4:17, 23 paraphrased).

Luke records it this way: "Fear not, from henceforth thou shalt catch men" (Luke 5:10). Now why this mention of fear? It is because at the command of Jesus these professional fishermen had lowered their nets into an "empty" sea and were stunned when they filled two boats to the sinking point with fish—a multitude of fish such as they had never seen. This incredible harvest is what Jesus said would happen if they followed Him and day after day lowered their nets into the world of men. The book of Acts and the rest of history record the blessed results of those who followed Christ in the adventure of missions, and the emptiness of those who did not.

Jesus began His missionary ministry by commanding fishermen to lower their nets as an object lesson of what was to come, and He ended His three years with them by uttering these significant last words, "All power is given unto me in heaven and in the earth. Go ye therefore and teach [disciple] all nations . . . teaching them to observe all things whatsoever I have commanded you; and lo, I am with you always, even unto the end of the world. Amen" (Matthew 28:18-20).

This final command and the promise of Jesus' power and presence extends down to us at the end of time.

> **The mission still stands:**
> the job is still uncompleted,
> and the reason we have been left here
> is to carry out the mission given to Jesus,
> and now passed on to us.

A Pattern for Our Commission

How then are we to carry out our commission?

Perhaps the best instruction in this regard comes from the pattern of Jesus' own life of mission.

1. Jesus' pattern involved a **corporate witness**. He gathered a group of men around Him who became a true community. They were to be a city set on a hill modeling the teachings of Jesus. This visible, corporate community was intensified after the resurrection, as we see in the book of Acts. Multitudes of people came to see for themselves what God was doing and to join. It was on this corporate body that He poured out His Spirit and gave a variety of gifts so the job could be done. Likewise, today, the responsibility *does not* fall on any one man, but upon all of us together. Community and missions belong together.

   There are many Hutterite colonies in my vicinity. They are often very successful in farming and manufacturing because the resources of many families and businesses can be tapped to ensure that the enterprises of the whole community are advanced. Think what impact could occur if true Christian communities could be established in many places to model the unity, love, and life of God, to prepare laborers, and to send out bands of missionaries near and far. What if all the

Consequences
of Ignoring Pillar 10:

Results of neglecting the call to be a missions community:

- *Individuals follow their own call, independent of the church.*

- *Laborers are not grounded in a kingdom perspective of Christianity, and so tend to share a liberal gospel.*

- *The church becomes more afraid of missions because it seems to lead to liberalism.*

- *Individuals not gifted in evangelism feel guilty because they don't know what to do for God.*

- *We use our resources for our own pet projects.*

- *We complain about little things because we don't see the big picture or the urgency of God's mission.*

- *The fire goes out.*

- *The people give themselves to materialism.*

families and businesses in your church banded together and used their gifts and resources for kingdom advance? What if they saw that as the primary business to which all their church and community activities pointed?

The whole church has been given the greatest job on earth. That job is not complete until believers are gathered and joined together in the new society of the church. That society is conscious in every aspect of life that her calling is missions. She is a community of light bringing glory to God.

Jesus' pattern of witness begins and ends with the mission community.

2. Jesus' pattern also involved **teaching** the life and values of heaven. He taught about what God expected in real-life situations. He spent three years investing in twelve men. Paul, the apostle to the Gentiles, also taught specific men and commissioned them to pass on a common deposit of the faith to other faithful men, who in turn would teach others (2 Timothy 2:2). He chose to stay in Ephesus for two years teaching in the school of Tyrannus and as a result, all Asia heard the Gospel. This was obviously no ordinary Bible school. *Teaching* and *going* went hand in hand.

Doing missions according to the pattern of Jesus means going into our Judea, Samaria, and the ends of the earth teaching what He taught.

3. Thirdly, Jesus' mission had a **prophetic** dimension. He came with a message of hope to the poor and to those who saw their need. He came with strong words for the rich, the powerful, and the self-sufficient. He came to bring in the acceptable year of the Lord—that is, the Jubilee of setting the oppressed free (Leviticus 25). He did this, not by political action, but by bringing forgiveness, confidence, peace, and thankfulness to the inner man. He did not just rearrange man's outer economic and political situation for the better. Rather, He changed the heart and attitude of

the man himself. He began at the bottom with the needy and not at the top with the influential.

Jesus did not attempt to reform the old society. Instead, He exposed its faulty foundation, took the axe to the root of the tree, and proclaimed the values of the kingdom of God as the foundation for His new society. The prophetic mission of Jesus and of the early church inaugurated what the world considered to be an upside down way of life. If we are to model missions after the pattern of Jesus, the end result must be the creation of an upside down people. To merely improve man's life in this present world falls short of the mandate of Jesus.

Notice that Jesus did not build a compound and hide from society. Neither should we, the new society of God's kingdom people, withdraw from the surrounding world with a "Berlin wall" around us. Rather, we are to be visible and vocal mission communities. We are a pilgrim people here whose ministry is that of our Master who came to salvage the world and call it back to the life (intimately knowing Him), the truth (submitting to His authority) and the way (following His pattern of life). Missions is prophetic. It is about restoring and fulfilling what God originally intended on this earth. This is not done through protests, through confronting the world, or by means of political action, but by quietly and consistently teaching and modeling the godly alternatives.

For instance, we may speak about the evils of abortion, but that should not be our emphasis. Instead, we lift up the biblical model of godly family life as a real possibility for each family. We give instructions and guidelines to parents to help them make this blessing a reality. We teach and live a lifestyle that is very different than the world in terms of the roles of males and females, moral purity, courtship, modesty, nonconformity, and Christian economics. We sing, visit, and minister together as families both in the church and in the community. We dare to be salt and light by together tackling such subjects as technology, movies, and media. Others may scorn our way of life, particularly those in the larger church, but we simply keep coming back to the Word of God as our guide. Together, we keep asking how we can apply it to the situations of our lives in a way that brings fruit. As we discover answers for life, we want to pass them on. We want to publicly teach, write, and witness in a way that presents this godly option and lifestyle to the families and society around us. It is still needful to publicly cry out as Peter did, "Save yourselves from this untoward [corrupt] generation" (Acts 2:40).

Too often the missionary adopts the culture because he forgets the profoundly prophetic dimension of Jesus' teaching.

In the Anabaptist church we need to accept that our distinctive call in missions is to embrace the prophetic dimension of Jesus' missionary activity. Our call in missions is not to just follow the evangelical "say a little prayer" understanding of evangelism, but to sound forth a serious call that invites people in the world and in the church back to the separated life and fellowship that God planned for His people from the beginning. We must stop apologizing for this prophetic message. Instead, we must more clearly define and embrace "who God has called us to be." We must more purposefully proclaim our distinctive kingdom message to the world. Prophets are not popular because the salt stings and the light exposes error, but once their message has taken effect, the end result is the preservation and manifestation of all that is good. The church—God's prophetic mission community—is to make visible the glorious reality of God's kingdom now.

Jesus' pattern of ministry in missions was distinctively prophetic. We remember Him today not because He was a nice person who tried to fit in with everyone, but because He dared to speak with prophetic authority to the issues of life.

4. Finally, Jesus had a **plan** to reach every place. He did not just sit

still; He went, as we are now to go. Many tried to get Him to settle down, to stay around their area, but He would not. He was compelled to go because that was what His Father had given him to do. "I *must* preach the kingdom of God to other cities also, for therefore am I sent" (Luke 4:43). Likewise, in Luke 8:1 we read, "He went throughout every city and village, preaching and shewing the glad tidings of the kingdom of God, and the twelve disciples were with him."

Later, in what is known as the mini-commission, or the practice commission, Jesus sent His disciples to teach and heal and live by faith as He had done: "And they departed, and went through the towns preaching the gospel and healing everywhere" (Luke 9:6; Luke 10:1-11; Matthew 9:35, 10:1-15).

It is clear that Jesus instituted a **strategic plan** to prepare laborers and to get the message out. The question for Jesus and His disciples was not, "Will they accept what we have to say?" Rather, it was, "Have they heard the message of the kingdom yet?" They *went everywhere to make sure that all had heard*. If they were rejected, they dusted off their feet and went on to the next town. Paul followed this same model.

A few years ago, another elder and I conducted an experiment which we called "The Six-Week Challenge." We sent out an invitation calling for twelve young men and two families who were willing to try to follow the example of missions left by Jesus and His disciples, as recorded in Matthew 10 and Luke 10. Our intent was to set aside six weeks in the summer to go from town to town looking for "worthy men" (Matthew 10:11) or seekers, just as the disciples had done.

First, those who responded gathered together for ten days. During this time, the two teams knit their hearts, prayed, and searched the Scriptures to get a clearer understanding of what the kingdom message was. We talked about the needs of our society, especially those of the modern day church, and went on some trial expeditions. Then each team went out for a month, living in tents and trusting God to lead them and to provide for their daily needs—and He did.

No one told the teams what to do or where to go. They had to get out their maps and pray. By faith they went forth searching for seekers to encourage, and in answer to that faith, God led them directly to hungry people every day. Through it all, their faith and excitement kept growing.

At the end, we gathered at a campground to report and discuss what could be done to follow up in these areas and mobilize a continual force of laborers. We had dreams and visions, but the smog of work demands and local church needs clouded them out.

How is it, brothers and sisters, that the clear command and example of Jesus and His disciples so easily gets *set aside* as we carry on with our own all-consuming agendas? Something is wrong. *We must repent* and seek His face. We have been given a commission. It begins now, and it begins here at home in our own country.

Jesus' pattern involved purposeful strategy and intensive preparation of workers.

Go Now—What About You and Your Church?

Jesus' pattern of preparing disciples who will themselves make disciples seems to be more of an apprenticeship, rather than seven years of seminary. This apprenticeship, involves both study and practical work right from the start.

It is easy to criticize those who spend years in academic study preparing for future ministry, but have we fallen into the same trap of preparing now and obeying later? Perhaps we have adopted the philosophy that we must first build a strong, united church with no problems or needs and then reach out to others. But consider with me, would you apply that idea in your business? No, if you drank coffee and built unity every day you would soon go broke and get on each other's nerves. In the workplace, team building, training, problem solving, and work go hand in hand, and so it should be in the church.

The clear call is to **go,** to begin at home in our Jerusalem and then to scatter and launch out from there to the ends of the earth (Luke 24:47; Acts 1:8). The early disciples failed to do this. They were so engrossed in the immensity of the work in Israel that they never left, and God sent great persecution to scatter them.

It is easy to stay in our Jerusalem, our comfort zone. The needs there are great, but the Master left us with a **specific command,** and one day He is coming again to see if we have done our part. This command violently interrupts the plans we have for our lives and businesses. The call to missions shakes us up; it is not comfortable. It totally rearranges our priorities, and our ideas of why we are left here on this earth.

Many in our land have heard of Jesus, but have they heard the Gospel of the kingdom? Have they been taught and called to obey the actual commands of Jesus? Has anyone gone to every city, town, and village? *Are the young people in your family and church growing up knowing that going out with the Gospel is a way of life?* Are they growing up anticipating the day that they will be sent out on a mini-commission to nearby provinces or states? Is it *clear* in your fellowship that you have picked up the torch of God's mission and that a spreading fire is going forth from you? Are you purposefully strategizing, training, and going, in order to fulfill the one great job that Jesus passed on to His church?

Prepared Laborers: The Missing Link

The great missing link in much of Anabaptist missions today is this purposeful preparation, mobilization, and support of laborers. We Anabaptist-type groups have been good at doing relief work, cleaning up after hurricanes, re-building barns, and helping with medical expenses. Our labor (time) and money are poured into these projects and into schools to educate our children. We have excelled at these social ministries, but why has not even more time and money been expended proclaiming the Gospel of the kingdom in every place, beginning in our own countries? We claim to have the foundational pillars of the faith that all must hear, but we leave the job of proclaiming the faith to the Protestants (who we say, have largely missed the critical kingdom message). That makes no sense.

We have prided ourselves in having no salaried ministers in our churches as if somehow not having paid workers will earn us a special "Well done" from the Lord. I know this is a sensitive subject with no easy answers, but maybe it needs to be examined. The final issue is not: "Are workers paid?" but rather: "Is the job God gave us being done?" To get the job done will take an army of trained, Spirit-filled volunteers as well as men who are released to give large portions of their time to equipping laborers and advancing the message and ministry of the kingdom. Why have we left this job to zealous individuals and to the rich among us? It is not the independent individual who has been commissioned with this great job, but the whole church. The church must get a vision of the work to which she is called, and then discern how her labor force can be equipped and supported to get the job done. To get the job done is going to take both *sacrifice* and *support*.

A few examples might help you see what I mean. Seven years ago, an inner city school was birthed in our province by young people who were confronted with the need. Many young people have given up years of their lives to serve as teachers, other young men recently created the "Hungry Teachers Fund" to help support them, and churches have given to pay for rent, mortgages, and buses. Slowly, the sacrifice of a few young people and one family who moved to the city has evolved into a joint sacrifice of several churches. This year the decision was made to move a man with a family to the city to serve as a fulltime supported principal. Is he a hireling? I hope not. I think he and his family are an answer to prayer—the prayer that the Lord of the harvest would call and send forth laborers into the harvest field. May we see many more workers released as the church gets involved sacrificially in the harvest and in fervent prayer. Frankly, we are better at supporting intensive missions when they are overseas then we are close to home, but missions begins at home. The church is a missionary community in which we all together seek to sacrifice and support so that the kingdom is advanced, beginning right here close to home. As long as missions is mainly something that happens far away it will never be a vital part of the life of the church.

As I have traveled, encouraging believers, I have been burdened with the need to see men who could be released and commissioned by the church to travel and give large portions of their time to evangelism and encouragement of scattered seekers and churches. Some years ago the administrator of a large tape ministry told me they receive many calls from people across the country who have been impacted by messages on serious Christianity and are requesting someone to visit and help them. I cannot forget his response: "We have no one to send."

To get a job done, you must know what the end goal or purpose is. (I.e. a warehouse business could state that its purpose is to stockpile, cut to size and deliver carpet and linoleum to stores or jobsites within two hours of receiving the order.) To do this there must be a mastermind behind the whole enterprise. There must be a warehouse, forklifts, workers, certified forklift drivers, and happy customers. If they only have one trained forklift driver, they will have a hard time fulfilling their objectives as a company and keeping their clients happy. So, what must they do? It's quite obvious. To get

> ## *Blessings*
> ### *of Embracing Pillar 10:*
>
> *Benefits of the church as a missions community:*
>
> - *The church is a community that has a purpose.*
> - *The church is continuously preparing workers with a foundation of kingdom teaching and living.*
> - *We know what we are passing on.*
> - *We are unashamed to be a prophetic community.*
> - *Everyone in the church unites and takes responsibility to get the job done.*
> - *Our resources are available for kingdom advance.*
> - *Families get excited about serving God.*
> - *Young people have something to give themselves to.*
> - *We joyfully submit to godly standards because we see the big picture and are engaged in the battle.*
> - *There is an environment of expectancy.*

the job done, they need to train a continual stream of forklift drivers. As kingdom Christians we believe the church has been given a job. To do this job, we need a continual stream of prepared laborers.

The blessed heritage of the Anabaptists places the responsibility to accomplish this job onto the whole church, not just the professional clergy. There is no clergy hired from afar to come and do the job for us. Instead, ministry is raised up from within and usually remains there for life, or until sent out by the church. There is great potential as a whole community of faith takes responsibility for the work. There is incredible potential, but all too often we have failed to embrace a specific purpose to which to give ourselves, and though we raise up laborers from within, we have failed to train them and to raise up enough to get the job done. No business would prosper and expand if it were run this way.

Please note that I am talking in this pillar about missions and about purposefully releasing laborers into the harvest field. We have pastors and deacons ordained to care for the flock, but missions is what happens outside the flock. Who in our churches has been given the responsibility to oversee the advance of the kingdom beyond the local church? Who has God set apart and gifted for this? How can they be supported to free them to do the job? We ordain pastors and deacons, but what about evangelists, traveling teachers, apostolic church planters, and men with prophetic ministries to the whole church or society? Why have we focused so much on those ministers that serve in the local church and neglected to equally recognize God's call for ministers who serve beyond the local body? Why do we put the responsibility for both pastoring and outreach all on one man, the pastor?

In the book of Acts we see that there are apostles such as Peter, Paul, and Barnabas who are given to missionary outreach, and there are helpers such as Timothy and Titus. Then there is another group, the elders of the local church. These two groups of leaders work together but have two distinct areas of gifting and responsibility. One Brethren denomination recognizes this distinction and ordains self-supporting elders who serve the local church, but also sets apart Gospel workers who live by faith and give themselves to evangelism, discipling, and outreach. The more intensely one is involved in ministry and outreach, the more difficult it will be to hold a fulltime, secular job.

Getting the Job Done

The question we will one day have to answer is: Did we get the job done? We must prepare and release laborers both inside the church and outside, so that the whole job of both missions and pastoring is faithfully carried out.

My dear brother minister, is preparing your people for ministry and mission at the center of your thinking, preaching, and discussions as a ministry team?

These realities must not be missing. They are our mandate. We dare not be too busy in our own work and miss God's last command. This pillar is not for later when we are mature or have resolved all the problems and needs in our Jerusalem. No, this pillar is for now. It must be there from the beginning. It is why we are still here. Without it, the building will sag and collapse.

"The harvest truly is great, but the laborers are few. Pray ye, therefore, the Lord of the harvest that he would send forth laborers into his harvest" (Luke 10:2; Matthew 9:36-38).

MEMORY AID

Pillar 1	**Who God Is** $\Big\{$	- A God of Intimate Communion
Pillar 2		- A God Who Speaks
Pillar 3		- Prophetic People
Pillar 4		- Upside Down Citizens
Pillar 5	**Who We Are to Be**	- Followers of Christ
Pillar 6		- New Creatures in Christ
Pillar 7		- Faith-Filled
Pillar 8		- Daily Dying
Pillar 9	**Governing Structure**	- It Helps Accomplish the **Be**ing and **Do**ing
Pillar 10	**What We Are to Do**	- Go into the Harvest Field in Jesus' Name
Pillar 11	**Counterfeits**	- The Call to Watchfulness

Seeds of the Faith—Pillar 11

The faith stands as mighty pillars, solid and unchanging. It rises as glorious mountain peaks, but it began its work in me as little seeds.

Missions means warfare. When we embrace missions, we will face great mountains, fierce storms, and a very real devil. Wherever something is attempted for God, distractions and counterattacks of the enemy are bound to occur.

Many of the classic books I read as a teenager dealt with the problem of good and evil. I had studied what the Bible says about evil. Out witnessing, I had even been chased by angry men with guns, but nothing prepared me for the evil I was to encounter as I entered the pastoral ministry.

I remember the time I unglued my ear from a two-hour phone call. The intensity of those hours had seemed like moments. For that short time, nothing else on earth existed. I didn't know it then, but I had just had my first direct encounter with evil. There have been many encounters since with evil, with the occult, with sin, with false teachers, with despisers of authority, and with divisive powers of darkness. The full strength of the missions warfare can hardly be understood until one has been on the front lines.

As I think of engaging in this warfare, my mind goes back over forty years to five young men in a canoe desperately fighting a fierce storm on Lake Winnipeg. The three miles across the bay didn't seem like much when we set out, but hours later we were in the dark and still only halfway there. I can still feel the all-absorbing intensity as every muscle was strained to the limit. If even one of us had stopped paddling for a moment, we would have lost control of our canoe and faced certain death. So we paddled as one man against an enemy, and we won.

I know something of storms, of evil, of the enemy, and of the cost of battle. I also know the devastation when God's people fight against flesh and blood instead of facing into the storm and fighting the real enemy.

A little seed is being planted in me of one people, standing arm-in-arm with a common mission and a common foe, a people with eyes to see the storm and the courage to paddle together as one man, with one Lord, one faith, and one mission.

◆

PILLAR 11

Watchfulness

We believe the church is called to a watchful warfare mentality. The Scriptures indicate everywhere the danger of deception and the need for discernment.

False Truth and False Anointings

The job of the Old Testament priest was, in part, to help the people discern between good and evil. The prophet Malachi tells us that in days of danger and deception, those who fear God and are concerned will speak "often one to another." Then the Lord will hear and cause that group of seekers to "*return, and discern* between the righteous and wicked, between him that serveth God and him that serveth him not" (Malachi 3:15-18; 2:17).

The religious people in Malachi's day were calling evil people good. They were blessing those who disregarded God. As they saw it, the fact that people prospered and were not judged by God proved that God delighted in their lives. Because of this, proud people were admired, unrighteous people were put in places of influence, and those who deliberately went against God's commands were declared to be saved (Malachi 2:17, 3:15).

This sounds so much like the confusion of our own day. In fact, people of every age have a desire for God, but they so easily choose a god made in their own image—one that tickles their ears with nice words and approves of how they live. It is this ear-tickling god, made to please man, who many times is preached in place of Christ.

An *anti-Christ* is something that is *against Christ* or *opposed to Christ*, but it also is something that is *in place of Christ*. It replaces Him with something that looks similar. Today, we call this a counterfeit. God told us that there will be many anti-Christ's (many counterfeit Christs) in the last days.

This word anti-Christ refers to a person who is literally coming at the end of time, falsely bearing the actual name of Christ. However, not every anti-Christ will claim to be the literal Christ. In fact, I have met only one person who claimed to be Jesus.

Take note, the word Christ also means *anointed,* so there will be *false anointings, false representations* of Christ and His message. There will be *counterfeit representations* of what Christ is like and what His message is. The danger for which we are to be on guard, then, is not just persons calling themselves the Christ, but also the dynamic, anointed ministers and ministries that claim to minister in the name of Christ, yet in practice go against His life and commandments. We are warned that these false teachers, false prophets, and false anointings will number in the multitudes (Matthew 7:15, 21-23; 1 Timothy 4:1-2, 6:3-5; 2 Timothy 3:1-7; 2 Peter 2:1-3,13-22; Jude; 1 John 2:18-20).

Setting a Standard That Makes Impurity Okay

Jude 1:4 declares that "certain men have crept in unawares ... ungodly men, turning the grace of God into lasciviousness" (i.e., a license to be impure). It is not necessarily that these people have intentionally come in to pervert the faith. Rather *they want the stamp of God's approval for their actions.* They want *the way they live to be the spiritual Christian norm* (or standard). They have not submitted to God's Word. Instead, they seek to make God's Word and God's people *fit in with their own experience.*

They have, so to speak, a high-gloss spiritual finish on their lives to cover over their true values. Paul says that these people have been deceived and are now deceiving others (2 Timothy 3:13).

We need to remember that behind all this deception and confusion lies a spirit of wickedness. It is "the working of Satan with all power and signs and lying wonders, and all deceivableness and unrighteousness in them that perish; because they received not the love of the truth, that they might be saved. And for this cause God will send them strong delusions, that they should believe a lie" (2 Thessalonians 2:9-11).

In light of this perilous war zone, Jesus warned His disciples before their first mini-mission that He was sending them out "as sheep in the midst of wolves; be ye therefore wise as serpents and harmless as doves" (Matthew 10:16). Two things are clear: the believer needs wisdom and discernment to stay alive, and he must not take on the nature of the wolf, but that of the dove.

Observations

Let me make a few observations about these warnings concerning deception and our need for watchfulness:

Consequences
of Ignoring Pillar 11:

When watchfulness is lacking:

- *We lose our communion with God.*
- *Our devotional times are unfulfilling.*
- *We lack wisdom and so make wrong choices.*
- *Our homes and church lack stability and order.*
- *Our people are gullible and fall prey to false and divisive teaching.*
- *We unwittingly open our lives to New Age spirituality and the occult.*
- *Obedience is renamed as legalism.*
- *We despise authority.*
- *There is little difference between the church and the world.*
- *Rebellion and immorality are tolerated and even expected.*
- *We return to our old sins and former ways.*
- *We cannot help the needy, so instead they begin destroying the church.*
- *A door is opened for Satan to destroy relationships.*
- *We fight with each other.*
- *We stop fellowshipping and start backbiting.*
- *Mountains of unforgiveness, hatred, and offenses seem to be unresolvable.*
- *Our best intentions and mission projects keep failing.*
- *Discouragement reigns.*
- *We enter a new "Dark Ages."*

1. Until now all the pillars we have considered have been positive. It seems out of place to introduce a negative pillar. But in actuality, it is not something I have introduced, for these warnings are consistent threads through all of Scripture and especially for these end times. It is imperative that we assume a warfare mentality of alertness and advance.

2. It struck me as I traced warnings and accounts of deception in the New Testament that two concepts often appeared together in the same context:

   a. The dangers of the false and counterfeit

   b. The need to uphold the Word, to hold on to what we have heard

   A treasure has been given to the believer. He has *already been given an anointing* and doesn't need a constant stream of new teachers and teachings (1 John 2:27). So, Jude 1:3 exhorts "that ye should earnestly contend for the faith which was once delivered unto the saints." The message of Jesus and His kingdom is simple. It is an old message, but as we discover it and live it, it becomes new every day!

3. Sometime ago as I was thinking on this topic, it took just a few minutes to jot down three pages of specific modern deceptions and emphases that take us on detours away from Christ and simple obedience to Him. Multitudes of things have been added to the faith or subtracted from it.

4. As I read the Sermon on the Mount (Matthew 5-7) it occurred to me that *the statements Jesus made counteract virtually every false teaching and deception that could confront us today!* We could never list all the deceptions, but we can read the red letters in our Bibles. We can take the Sermon on the Mount seriously as God's standard for us. We can live in such a way that anything opposed to this life and standard will be out of place and leave a warning stench in our nostrils. We can judge fruit as Jesus told us to.

A Positive Remedy

The Sermon on the Mount provides a positive remedy for the counterfeit dangers around us. It also provides a standard for measuring what is righteousness and what is unrighteousness. The last verses of this passage, Matthew 7:13-27, form a conclusion which emphasize:

- That only the few and not the many will follow this way

- That there will be much bad fruit, which indicates a bad tree

- That many will say "Lord, Lord," and speak of all they have done for God, but He will say, "I never knew you, depart from me ye that work iniquity" (7:21-23)

- That those who hear and do are building a spiritual house that will stand on the rock

Here then, is a vital pillar. We must press forward in the battle. We must "preach, reprove, rebuke, exhort… for the time will come when they will not endure sound doctrine; but after their own lusts shall heap to themselves teachers, having itching ears; and they shall turn away… unto fables. **But watch thou in all things**" (2 Timothy 4:3-7).

Brothers, I exhort you in these dangerous times to gather often, as did the seekers in Malachi's time, to consider the positive direction of God. If we do, He will give us discernment.

> ### *Blessings*
> *of Embracing Pillar 11*:
>
> *Benefits of watchfulness:*
>
> - *The church walks in wisdom and discernment.*
> - *The church is grounded on a solid foundation.*
> - *There is security and stability.*
> - *Holiness and separation are maintained.*
> - *We are able to guide the young people and strugglers instead of being led astray by them.*
> - *Satan is unable to destroy our communion and community.*
> - *The whole body unites to fight danger.*
> - *We identify and dethrone the idols of our day.*
> - *We love fruitfulness and the narrow way.*
> - *We advance together with faith and expect to see Satan falling and God's kingdom advancing.*

Seeds of the Faith—Pillar 12

The faith stands as mighty pillars, solid and unchanging. It rises as glorious mountain peaks, but it began its work in me as little seeds.

Until I began attending Bible School, I don't remember ever hearing anything about the end times. I do remember not being too excited about singing in the choir forever.

Slowly I began to realize that God's creation in this universe is very good. I saw that the purpose of God for the Christian man and woman is challenging and fulfilling. So the thought came, "How could heaven not be even greater and even more fulfilling?" I read in my Bible that he who is faithful with little responsibilities will be given greater responsibility when the Master returns.

Then, somewhere in those early years, I was intrigued by what E. Stanley Jones contemplated saying when he sees Jesus. It is something like this, "Lord, for me, the greatest thing on earth has been telling others of you. If you have some lost universe somewhere that has never heard of you, it would be heaven for me if you would send me there."

Through all these little seeds, a thought was planted: What if the things important to me now, help to determine what I will be doing through all eternity?

Serving, worshiping, and glorifying God—that is what life is to be here in our preschool for eternity. These activities are an even greater blessing through all eternity.

PILLAR 12

You Will Give Account

*We believe the church is to be watching
continually for the soon return of the Lord.
He is coming to separate the sheep and the
goats, and to judge and reward the faithfulness
of His people in the job He left us to do.*

Will He Find Faith?

In Luke 18, we read a parable Jesus told of a woman who, through her persistence was given justice by a worldly judge. Jesus says, "How much more will God avenge [do what makes things right] for believers who cry to Him." A day of making things right is coming, and the question in that day of the Lord's coming will be, (verse 8), "Shall He find faith on the earth?"

We have tried in this book to outline the big picture of God's design for His people. This big picture is what the faith is. It is how the faithful are now to live. It is an exposition and foundational survey of the pillars of a life of faith. The question is, **Will He find us living in a way that demonstrates our obedience to the faith?**

As we said at the beginning, we too often get lost in the noisiness and fog of modern existence, and we miss the great purpose of God. We forget that we were left here with a job to do. We were left to represent and model, here and now, the life of the kingdom of heaven, and also to advance the message of this kingdom into all the earth. In some way, we all have a part in this, and one day we each will give account as to how faithfully we fulfilled our part.

Let me ask, if your boss or your dad gives you a job to do while he goes away, who is it that will evaluate or judge how well you did? It will be the one who gave you the job. Can you excuse your disobedience by saying, "I forgot," "I got distracted," "I was too busy," "I was afraid of not doing a good enough job," "Everyone discouraged me," or "No one else was doing it either"? No!

A Day of Accounting Is Coming

Concerning the end of the age, Jesus said no man knows the hour. He clearly told us our part: "Take heed, watch and pray: for ye know not when the time is. For the Son of Man is as a man taking a far journey, who left his house and gave authority to his servants, and to every man his work, and commanded the porter to watch. Watch therefore, for ye know not when the master of the house cometh... lest suddenly coming, He find you sleeping. And what I say unto you, I say unto all, Watch" (Mark 13:33-37).

In another parable concerning faithfulness and accountability, Jesus pictured a master who has left a steward, or manager, to rule over all his affairs in his absence. He said, "Blessed is that servant whom his lord when he cometh shall find so doing. Of a truth I say unto you that he will make him ruler over all that he hath... And that servant who knew his lord's will and prepared not himself, neither did according to his will, shall be beaten with many stripes... For unto whomsoever much is given, of him shall be much required" (Luke 12:43, 44, 47, 48). Notice, this latter servant knew, but did not prepare. He knew, but did not act.

Perhaps the best-known story describing this day of reckoning is that of the talents in Matthew 25:14-30. A man going to a far country calls his servants and gives to each differing amounts of money (talents) with which to conduct the master's business. He gives to "every man according to his [God-given] ability" and on his return calls them for a time of reckoning (Matthew 25:14-30). To those who gained a profit, his lord says, "Well done, thou good and faithful servant, thou hast been faithful over a few things, I will make thee ruler over many things; enter thou into the joy of thy lord" (Matthew 25:21). The servant who never used the master's money for good has his money taken from him and given to others, and he is cast into outer darkness because of his disobedience.

Two themes appear over and over in Jesus' teachings:

- A day when the good and bad will be separated

- A day when a returning master will evaluate and reward the work of the servants that he left behind to do the work

> ## *Consequences*
> ### *of Ignoring Pillar 12:*
>
> *Results of ignoring the day of accounting:*
>
> - *I grumble about this present life.*
>
> - *I think about my body, my health, my stuff, my retirement, my rights, and about getting my just reward now.*
>
> - *I feel I'm not that bad. I have plenty of excuses for my spiritual inactivity.*
>
> - *I see all the failings of my brothers and my ministers.*
>
> - *The candle of the church goes out because she is hardened and does not accept God's present correction.*
>
> - *I have very little to do with my brothers and sisters.*
>
> - *I sense no urgency to encourage them.*
>
> - *I avoid God's judgment now, so it will be horrible later.*
>
> - *I appear holy and important now, but one day all will be revealed.*
>
> - *Ahead there is eternal death, agony, and separation from God.*

The Test of Fire

Paul also plainly teaches (1 Corinthians 3) that all men have been given responsibilities, some to plant and some to water, but that the work is all *one*—it is all for Christ and because of Christ. We are only "laborers together with God" (verse 9) and yet "every man shall receive his own reward according to his own labor" (verse 8).

He goes on to say that "every man's work shall be made manifest for the day shall declare it because it shall be revealed by fire; and the fire shall try every man's work of what sort it is. If any man's work abide which he hath built thereupon he shall receive a reward. If any man's work shall be burned, he shall suffer loss; but he himself shall be saved; yet so as by fire" (verses 13 and 14). "Therefore, judge nothing [as to who is greatest and most faithful] before the time, until the Lord come, who both will bring to light the hidden things of darkness and will manifest the counsels of the hearts and then shall every man have praise of God" (1 Corinthians 4:5).

A time of accounting, reward, or reproof is ahead for each of us. A time is coming when, in some manner, future and eternal responsibility will be given to the servants of the King. He has gone away, and we have been left with instructions relating to the big job He wants done. He is coming again when the time is completed, and He will be looking for the evidence of our faithfulness. To some who did much in their own strength and pride He will say, "I never knew you" (Matthew 7:21-23). To others who seemed to do little, He will offer great reward because they did what He gave them to do.

Blessings
of Embracing Pillar 12:

Benefits of living in light of a day of accounting:

- I am motivated to serve and suffer without present reward.
- I commit all the work and ministry of my life to Him who is able to keep it against that day.
- I am trusting God to work through my brother, and realize that the final judgment of his work rests with God, not with me.
- I live continuously ready for His coming.
- We daily stir one another up to love and good works.
- Others may misjudge me or persecute me now, but true judgment is ahead.
- Judgment and discipline begins with the church now if she is able to hear and repent.
- I can be corrected now instead of being punished later.
- Eternal life has begun.
- Life is filled with faith, expectancy, and joy as I serve in His kingdom now.
- There is no fear of death.
- I don't know all that is ahead, but if this life is just kindergarten for eternity, then it must be good.

The Exam Is Coming

My friend, you and I are not ignorant—we have been told about a day of accounting. We have been told on what basis we will be examined. I fear lest somehow we as individuals and the church live our lives as if this exam is not ahead for us. When He comes, will He find faith on the earth?

MEMORY AID

Pillar 1 ..... COMMUNION— **God exists** ⎱ Who God Is

Pillar 2 COMMUNICATION—**God has spoken**
Pillar 3 ..... COMMUNITY— **Peoplehood**
Pillar 4 ...... CITIZENSHIP— **The Kingdom of God** ⎱ Who
Pillar 5 ... COMMITMENT— **Discipleship** We Are
Pillar 6 ..... CONVERSION— **The New Birth** to **Be**
Pillar 7 ...... CONFESSION— **Faith**
Pillar 8 . CROSS-BEARING— **Humility**

Pillar 9 .... CHURCH— **Ecclesia**—
The Practical Governing Structure to Help Us:

Become God's Model People
–and–
Do the Work of the Kingdom

Pillar 10 ... COMMISSION— **Missions** ⎱ What We Are to **Do**

Pillar 11 ... COUNTERFEIT— **Watchfulness**
The Opposition to Being and Doing

Pillar 12 .... COMING— **You Will Give Account**
Examination of Fruit and Works

Which U-Boat Are You In?

Why then do you exist? Imagine for a moment that you and your church are a U-boat, one that has personality and the power of choice. To you is given the choice to be a U-boat in battle out on the seas or one in a museum. Which would you choose?

In the preceding chapters, we have explored the panoramic, big picture of that which God intended for His church—His U-boat. But you have a choice, for there are two distinctly different models of the faith. The twelve pillars we have examined form a foundation or skeleton for understanding and promoting the faith from the perspective of the kingdom Christianity pursued by the Anabaptists and other Radical Believers' Churches. Just as the crew on a U-boat in battle needs to know the purposes and expectations of the Captain, so, we as God's crew must know what He is doing and expecting if we are to fulfill our part and discover the beauty of why we exist.

Seeds of the Faith

The faith stands as mighty pillars, solid and unchanging. It rises as glorious mountain peaks, but it began its work in me as little seeds.

When my daughter left home to teach school, I inherited her herb garden. Actually, the garden also was home to strawberries, rhubarb, roses, and lots of other flowers. There was a bench, and an arbor, a sundial, and paths between all of the little garden plots. I wasn't able to identify everything that grew there. Some of the plants grew eight feet tall and spread their seed all through the lawns and pastures. Other things could hardly be persuaded to grow at all. Many times I dug up the hard, gumbo clay soil and added peat moss and manure. The work and the weeding never ended, and somehow the garden never did seem quite finished, but that didn't matter. I still loved being there.

For one whole summer after we moved, our little farm sat empty, and the herb garden was neglected and became wilder than ever. One evening while I was there mowing lawns, two sisters drove up to look at the house. They got out of the car and headed straight for my overgrown herb garden. I don't know what they thought of the house, but they loved my garden. No, I guess it was God's garden. I hadn't done anything to give those flowers their glory. I hadn't even done my part in caring for them, but God never stopped doing His part.

An underlying seed that has been at work in my life is the simple belief that God is at work. He is building His people. His design for His people is not doom, defeat, or monotony. It is faith, life, and revival. Deep inside, I know that God is at work and He will be glorified.

We live in dark and confusing days. There's so much to do in God's garden that we hardly know where to start. We know the work will never end. If we just look at this earthly picture, we could have reason to despair, but there is a big picture. There is a God at work. He has a glorious plan and design for the garden He is growing. His glory will fill all the earth.

The Marriage of Spiritual and Practical

In these pages I have only hinted at all the practical out-workings and applications of the twelve pillars. I have desired rather to lay out the underlying structure in a way that I hope will help you see the big picture, and in light of that vision be able to talk together and seek God concerning the specific parts that become the meat on the bones and the energy of the body. However, I realize that many of you, like me, are struggling in this matter of how to deal with the practical applications and our failures in them. I therefore added these few thoughts concerning "GOD and this world's stuff," or put another way, concerning the spiritual and the practical, or God and standards. I hope that it helps to stimulate some thoughts.

Pillar "A-to-Z"

**We believe that God is the Beginning and the End,
and that the end is a new beginning.**

And I heard a great voice out of heaven saying,
> *Behold the tabernacle of God is with men,*
> *and he will dwell with them,*
> *and they shall be his people,*
> *and God himself will be with them,*
> *and be their God.*
>> *And God shall wipe away all tears from their eyes;*
>> *and there shall be no more death, neither sorrow, nor crying,*
>> *neither shall there be any more pain:*
>> *for the former things are passed away.*

And he that sat upon the throne said,

> *Behold I make all things new.*

And he said unto me,

> *Write: for these words are true and faithful.*

And he said unto me,

> *It is done.*
>
> *I am the Alpha and Omega,*
>
> *the beginning and the end.*
>
> *I will give to him that is athirst of the fountain of the water of life freely.*
>
> *He that overcometh shall inherit all things;*
>
> *and I will be his God,*
>
> *and he will be my son. (Revelation 21:3-7)*

In the Beginning, God; in the End, God

This isn't a new pillar. Really, it is the only pillar, the one that sums up all the others. Having considered all that fills these pages, we come back to the beginning—God exists; He is central to all; He is the Beginning and the End, the Alpha and Omega (A and Z).

I hadn't planned to write this chapter, but I can't get away from the realization of how utterly small I am, how utterly small this book is, and how utterly small all the statements of faith, all the books man has written, and all of man's ministry and efforts truly are. Unless God is central, none of this makes sense. We can't figure it out and then do it. We can't just set a new high standard or vision and think that somehow now we can live it. God must be central. He must be our all. He must be our passion. I cannot for a moment presume to be able to build His church. That is His job. I cannot protect His church. I cannot build enough statements or standards to keep the people in and the devil out. I cannot open the doors wide enough to get others in to the kingdom. I cannot manufacture the moving of the Spirit. I cannot convince a soul concerning the uselessness and illusion of all this world's treasures, nor concerning the priority of laying up heavenly treasure. It has to be God; *He has to be **big***. He has to come in His glory, and for that we must seek Him.

I believe we need a high and holy standard far higher than what we have. We need a far greater commitment to serve and give our all in His work—note, I said—in *His* work and when we work, we get tired. We need a high standard, and we also need to get to the work, but these are just what we do. They are not our focus. **Our focus is Him**. He is our glory. He is the One we worship in all of life.

What then of the standard and the call to work? Why is there so much reaction against standards? Why are we so reluctant to give up the little things of this world that we value? Is it not because God has become small, and the things have become big? *When God is **big**, all other things become small!* Remember the dog in the park? Where does he run? To admire the beauty? No, to the garbage can, and he will collect all he can. What about us? Is our focus on the garbage of self-pursuit and this world's values and stuff, or have we, like Paul the Apostle considered all that as dung, that we may win Christ? (Philippians 3:8). Why do we say no to a holy standard, and say yes to the questionable standards and garbage the world offers us? It is because the standard that calls us higher has become the dung, and that standard which the world presents has become the gold. One brother put it aptly when he said,

> *"When the glory of God is present, no standard is too high; but when the glory of God is gone, all standards become odious."*

Set It and Forget It

I suggest that we need to *set a high standard*, and then, in a sense, forget about it and focus on Christ, talk of Christ, and commune around Christ. *The standard simply sets some things in order so we don't need to always be thinking about them and talking about them, and thus can give ourselves to worshiping and serving Christ.*

When we lose our brotherly agreement and each one does what is right in his own eyes, our focus and conversation *shifts* away from Christ and

His work and on to each other and the differing standards, or lack of them. We end up dividing into liberal and conservative camps, when, in reality, the problem is that somehow we have both been distracted away from Christ. The glory has gone, and we are striving with each other. Some claim to be in Jesus' camp and don't even want to talk of these external things. But this, too, misses the heart of the issue—God's presence is gone, and that is why we cannot talk. You see, God has commanded us to talk about all things, to relate our faith to all of life, and to come to a place of one-minded agreement as a brotherhood so we can be undistracted by continual controversy, divisive distractions, and evil speaking. Can I propose an experiment for those brotherhoods who are unable to talk and agree on standards or even a vision? Here it is:

> Why not simply adopt the highest standards possible from churches or brothers you respect and agree to all keep them for two years and not to talk unnecessarily about them or complain about them? Those who cannot, can gracefully leave or be visitors/seekers. *During that time, put much focus on your fellowship with Christ and with each other, and much energy into His service,* and then after two years come together to evaluate and give ownership to your own vision and standards.

Let me give two little stories to back this up:

Once a brother told me he thought it would be good if we all could, so to speak, "be under the law" for six months. Now that sounds a little "off" or strange, but what he meant was that we often get into bad habits in our lives and that if we could just all submit to some positive habits (e.g., weekly corporate prayer, a weekly hospitality night, no radio) and practice them long enough, we would not want to go back to the old ways—we would see the fruit!

I have never forgotten the testimony of another brother who had been impacted by a Radical Believers'-type of church. Specifically, he saw three distinctive things in this group that made it different from evangelical Christianity as he had observed it. Those three areas of difference were what he calls "The Three M's"—modesty, marriage, and music. He deeply respected the witness and teaching of this group, but was skeptical of their position on music. He therefore reasoned that because he saw the truth and fruit of their message in other areas, he was not going to react because he could not understand one area. Instead, he decided to assume that their strong position could be right in this area, too. So he decided to put away all his music for two years, focus on growing in the Lord, and then at the end of two years, bring it out again and seek to discern which was good and which was not. You may have already guessed the result. He acquired new discernment and convictions and was able to discard much of his old music.

Marriage of the Practical and the Spiritual

The reason I share these things is very simple. Many of our churches are trapped in a tug of war between the spiritual and the practical. We put the related issues at opposite ends of a long line and assume that they cannot come together. My reading and observation suggest that many of us who become the "revived" hesitate to talk about or clarify practical things because we consider them to be unspiritual. In so doing, we actually keep a door open to the world, a door that should be firmly shut (and that certainly is unspiritual). When the door to the world is left swinging on its hinges, we lose our united prophetic voice and end up in two different camps within the church, each speaking against the other.

God's design is that the spiritual and practical be united as one. Neither will work without the other. We must first know how **big** God is and then submit one to another in little practical things so we can have a united witness and be calling each other to higher ground. Now that is spiritual.

All the pillars that we have discussed form a foundation or framework, a skeleton. If we get them established, then we have the groundwork laid for many of the daily decisions concerning the Christian life as well as the ministry and priorities of the church. But if we are afraid and fail to talk about the practical things, the building will be incomplete and will soon show signs of age.

We need a high standard—don't let it be you who drags it lower—and we need to get to the great work that has been left to us. But then we, in a sense, need to forget about both of these because they are very small, and ensure that the thrust of our whole lives is seeking and worshiping the God who is **big**.

Memory Aid

We exist to be God's distinct people (His crew) and to do His will.

The big kingdom picture gives us a foundational understanding of God's ultimate plan so we can find our small part in it, make wise decisions, and fulfill His will on earth as it is in heaven.

- Pillar 1—COMMUNION—**God exists**—Intimate Relationship
- Pillar 2—COMMUNICATION—**God has spoken**—Hear and Obey
- Pillar 3—COMMUNITY—**Peoplehood**—Prophetic Peoplehood
- Pillar 4—CITIZENSHIP—**The Kingdom of God**—The Upside Down Kingdom
- Pillar 5—COMMITMENT—**Discipleship**—Following Christ in Life
- Pillar 6—CONVERSION—**The New Birth**—Christ, the Door to Life
- Pillar 7—CONFESSION—**Faith**—Faith is the Key
- Pillar 8—CROSS-BEARING—**Humility**—Dying Daily
- Pillar 9—CHURCH—**Ecclesia**—The Relational, Governing Structure
- Pillar 10—COMMISSION—**Missions**—The Church's Task
- Pillar 11—COUNTERFEIT—**Watchfulness**—The Road is Narrow
- Pillar 12—COMING—**You Will Give Account**—The Exam is Coming
- MARRIAGE OF SPIRITUAL AND PRACTICAL—When God is big, the standard is high

Seeds of the Faith

The faith stands as mighty pillars, solid and unchanging. It rises as glorious mountain peaks, but it began its work in me as little seeds.

Identifying the pillars in this book didn't happen because I just sat down one day and studied hard, and then suddenly developed them. Rather, this kingdom view was birthed in the study, discoveries, and travail of a lifetime. The seeds were planted by God. There had been seasons of communion, of retreat, of community, of failure, and then finally clouds rolled back and I was captivated by the picture of majestic pillars of the faith that belong not to me, but to God. They were mighty pillars, ancient pillars, such basic and obvious pillars. Understanding them gave new meaning to all of life. Why then had no one ever told me of this Gospel of God's kingdom now?

Have the Clouds Been Rolled Back?

We have come to the end of our discussion explaining these twelve pillars of kingdom Christianity. I hope it will be just the beginning or a new beginning for you. I hope you will be part of a brotherhood that can unitedly say, "We believe…," and live it. I have not covered every point of doctrine. Much has been unsaid. I have attempted rather to give a framework for considering and teaching the faith. I have tried to give it a distinctively Anabaptist and radical order and approach.

If you were driving through Switzerland and missed seeing the Alps due to thick layers of cloud, I think you would be very disappointed. How much more devastating, if we as the church live under the anti-Christ clouds that hide or reduce the glory of the Gospel of the kingdom.

The New Testament warns us that the end times will be characterized by many clouds of counterfeit Christianity that darken the vision of the church. I hope that some of these clouds have been dispersed by the light of the big picture of God's design and purpose. I hope you have gotten a positive picture of what the faith is. It is not mainly a list of creeds and statements you confess and agree with. Rather, it is expressed in how you live.

The faith is seen not in print, but in action, in living letters, in cities of light set on a hill, in communities of the kingdom lived out here and now. Expressing the faith should not be like a list of facts about a U-boat in a museum. It should rather be like the instructions and inspiration of the commander to his crew as they go into action. I pray you will be inspired to new vision and action.

Perhaps you can take this study a step deeper by personalizing and memorizing the points in this book so that you can make them your own and use them in living room fellowship or discipling. (That would be better than talking about the crops or church problems.) If you are a dad, you could take these pillars and a list of the Scriptures and use them for teaching your children or young people. One family that reviewed this book for me gave me beautiful, laminated bookmarks with the twelve pillars and some pertinent questions on one side and some practical applications on the other!

If you are a minister, I encourage you to systematically teach the foundational pillars of the faith until you are confident that your people have seen God's heart and the big picture. If you can't do this kind of teaching, find someone who can and then keep building on it. Again, don't just preach on individual pieces of the doctrinal puzzle—tie them together. Keep the big picture always in your people's minds. Another thing I encourage you to do, is to study these pillars as a brotherhood, and get very practical about how they apply to you as a church. Don't stop with just a good Bible study. Make some actual decisions together about what you will do as a church to put what you have discovered into practice. The next chapter is an appendix with a list of questions that could be used to stimulate godly discussion and decision making.

Perhaps you could use these pillars as a launching pad for a distinctively Anabaptist and radical statement of faith for your church fellowship, or a tract explaining what you believe. Remember, the early Anabaptists wrote many tracts outlining their distinctive beliefs, and I don't think they were just dull lists. We need some modern-day statements and tracts that inspire people to want to be kingdom Christians.

Some readers may follow these suggestions and some readers may have other ways of implementing these foundational truths. In any case, please remember that my main desire has not been to give you more information or a list of statements to put in a drawer and forget. My prayer has been that some pillars of a radical faith can be established as a foundation in your lives and churches, and that as a result, you would have a clearer vision of

- Why you are here
- Where you are going
- Why you are different, and must be

My fear is that the pattern of life in the world and the pattern of modern Christian thinking are undermining the radical Anabaptist type of faith. So, again I pray that these pages will help you begin an ongoing dialogue, and that they will encourage you to purge, refocus, and reorganize what you believe, how you live, and how you make disciples.

Some of you are Anabaptist in background and struggling or even ashamed. I hope this helps. Some of you are evangelicals, Protestants, Charismatics, or Pentecostals. I know seeds of the kingdom have been planted in many of you. Many of you see the spiritual smog, and clouds and yearn to have them rolled back, so you as a church can live out the perfect will of God. My prayer is that you will be inspired to consider these kingdom pillars of the faith and that God will help you to take the next obedient steps to apply the truths of the kingdom beginning where you are right now. Finally, some of you are Jews, Muslims, Hindus, Buddhists, or materialists, or have no faith in God. For you, I pray that something of the beauty of Jesus and the dream He has for His people will capture your heart.

For all, I pray you will have a more radical commitment to God and to seeking ways of more faithfully living out your faith than when you began. Remember, God has been at work for six thousand years perfecting a people, and He hasn't given up. For this reason, I exhort you to keep on, for he that endures to the end shall be saved (Matthew 10:22, 24:13).

Seeds of the Faith

The faith stands as mighty pillars, solid and unchanging. It rises as glorious mountain peaks, but it began its work in me as little seeds.

Where do we go from here?

Did you notice the word we? *Great things have been done for God by great individuals. Their stories have inspired me. But as long as I can remember, I have wondered, "What could God do through a people fully consecrated to Him?" I knew there had to be a* we. *In Bible school, I studied the book of Acts. I saw that living churches kept growing and multiplying. I dreamed of planting a network of a hundred house churches joined together as one powerful multiplying unit. Ten years later, in the backwoods of Canada, a trapper and his wife came to God. Then one after another their relatives followed. It was a little taste of the multiplying that the early church experienced. A seed of hope was planted—this is what God wants. Maybe it can happen even in Canada.*

In another ten years, we found ourselves again and again in Gospel tent meetings with Hutterites, Mennonites, and other hungry seekers. We saw revival. Lives were changed. Churches were planted. Again, by the eye of faith, I could see a hundred churches in a generation. There was desire, there was revival, there was a hunger for truth, but when the hard times came, we faltered. We had failed to establish a united vision and a clear understanding of who we were and what we believed. We wanted life together, but we were afraid of the hard work of agreeing together. We faltered, and many of you have, too, but it's not over. Our people are tackling the hard work of coming to unity and agreement.

Churches that know what they believe, that stand in unity to pass on the common deposit, that are full of life—this is God's heart. Churches that multiply the life and the message of God's kingdom from place to place even in America; this, too is God's design.

Will a hundred churches rise up in a generation? I might not see it, but where men and women dare to ask kingdom questions, commit themselves to advance the kingdom, and are filled with the life of Christ, churches will begin to multiply.

Years ago, I had a seed, a vision, planted in my life of churches multiplying and standing together. It's still not fulfilled, but I think it's broader now than it was back then. I think it's part of God's dream, of God's design. It's not going to happen on its own. It can't be realized just by the efforts of strong leaders. For its fulfillment, the vision still depends on "we" who know how to agree.

APPENDIX:
Where Do We Go From Here?

Crucial Questions to Ask Together as a Church

These questions are given at the end of the book so that they can be answered in light of the whole teaching of these twelve pillars. They are designed to be asked as a church brotherhood or ministry team, perhaps at a weekend retreat. If the church is to have a life that is worth passing on, it must know who it is, what it believes, what it practices, why it exists. It must have a purpose. I hope these questions can help you clarify these important matters.

Asking and then living out the answer to these questions is a big job. It won't happen overnight. So first, *seek to come to some agreement as to where you want to be eventually.* Next, ask: *What are the first steps you can take to purposefully make your objectives a reality?* Finally, establish: *How will you keep the process going of moving towards a clearer and more purposeful church? How will you evaluate? Who will be responsible? When will they meet? Who will we be accountable to?*

The Call to Hear and Respond

One of the premises of this book is that we all fall short and have failed to live up to the expectations God has for His people, therefore we must hear what the Spirit is saying to the churches today. One of the ways we can do this is by together asking some penetrating questions concerning where we are at, what God is saying, and what action steps we ought to be taking. This is called *response*. As kingdom Christians we have said that we believe in hearing and doing; that means we believe in purposefully responding to what we have heard. So as the church seeks direction, she hears, she discusses, she decides, and she takes godly action. Too often we stop with hearing and talking, but our churches, our families, and our world are waiting for men who will dare to hear and act together.

Do we believe the Word of God is to be literally responded to and obeyed?

How well do we as a church discuss and make practical application relating to the issues of the day?

How could we do this better?

The Big Picture and the Clouds

Twelve times in this book I have stated, "We believe…," but, who is the we?

Do the pillars presented in this book represent the core of what we as a church believe, desire to build on, and want to pass on? (Don't just say yes. Take time to talk about the truth of each pillar.)

In which pillars are we weakest?

In which ones are we the strongest?

For each pillar, write out an objective of something you feel God is wanting for you as a church. What specific steps could we take towards making each pillar a living reality.

If the individual pieces of our Christian faith and our church practice are to make sense, it helps if we have seen the big picture of God's design. When we have isolated pieces of truth but no master picture, we tend to use spiritual saws, sledgehammers, and cutting torches to try to make the pieces fit, or to make the people accept them. This is moralism—the principles are good, but the people do not see the beautiful kingdom picture, so leaders end up seeking to enforce the truth in ways that are not good.

What must we as a church do to hold the big master picture of what we believe before the eyes of all the people?

What are the biggest obstacles or cloud layers that keep us as a church from living out the truths in these pillars of kingdom Christianity?

What Does It Mean to Be the Church?

I have said that Protestants and Anabaptists have two distinctively different understandings of the church.

Do we as a church understand these differences and are we making choices and practical applications accordingly?

What kind of church/ecclesia do we want to be?

In this book I have tried to lay a foundation, paint a big picture, or explore the skeleton on which flesh is placed and life breathed in. Now you as a church must build on that foundation, get specific about the working out the details of the picture, and make the applications that put flesh on the bones.

If you do not have a vision of these foundational things, the tendency will be to use leadership authority to enforce the right applications. In many revival settings there has been life and perhaps even some great principles, but an individualistic concept of the church is retained and thus it is difficult to agree on practical applications.

One of the premises of this book is that foundations come before applications. In other words, *we first settle if we believe in the doctrine of the two kingdoms, the doctrines of discipleship, ecclesia, missions, and the other foundational teachings, and only then can we fruitfully discuss the specifics such as modesty, music, marriage, and money.*

In light of this, here are some more foundational questions:

Who Makes Decisions and How Do We Make Them?

Who sets the direction, beliefs, and practices—the gathered church, or each individual and each home?

One of the biggest questions regarding the church is this: *Does the church have the authority and responsibility to make decisions and come to common agreements about practical areas of our lives?* In other words, *does the church teach principles and also make practical applications, or does she teach principles, and leave the applications to each family and each individual?*

If we as a brotherhood do not make the practical decisions and applications, who will?

If the applications are made by each individual or family, then what is the purpose of ministers and of the brotherhood?

Consider some of the change (drift) that has happened in our circles especially relating to practical applications. How were the decisions to make these changes made? Did they just happen, and now we don't know what to do? What can we learn from this? How can we do things differently?

Have we as a church decided how we decide? In our meetings do we have clear proposals, open discussion, and clear decisions, with conclusions about the action to be taken? Or is all of this vague? Are our decisions recorded and appropriately shared with the whole congregation? Is there good pastoral instruction and in-home teaching about the new direction? Or is it assumed that somehow everyone will know what is expected?

Have we as a church decided how we deal with sin, relational differences and differences of vision and practice? How well are we doing this? Is our most normal method of handling problems to use a cutting torch, the sledgehammer, the hiding place under the carpet, or to resolve issues openly and with a clear goal of reconciliation?

What are the role expectations of ministers and members?

What is the role of the ministers (apostles, prophets, evangelists, pastors, teachers, elders, bishops, deacons, etc.) in the gathered life, services, and decision-making process?

What is the role of the congregation in the gathered life, services, and decision-making process?

What is required before one is ordained as a minister?

How is a minister removed?

Who Is a Part?

What kind of commitment is required if a person is to be a functioning part (a member) of the life and decision-making of the local brotherhood?

What is expected before one is accepted as such a member?

How do we know who the members are?

How is a member removed?

Does someone become a member of the local church when they are converted, when they are baptized, or at a later point?

Are they expected to submit to discipling or catechizing before baptism, after baptism, or not at all?

What happens if a new member resists the direction of the church?

Are we as a church willing to pay the cost of discipling and correcting new and old members?

What practical steps can we take to improve our discipling of new members?

What Is the Place of Unity and Agreements?

Which is a greater struggle for us as a church: coming to agreement about the biblical principles, or coming to agreement about godly applications?

Do we have a brotherly agreement? If not, why not?

What does it mean to submit one to another and be of one accord? Is that practical or just spiritual?

American society and American Christianity have become very individualistic. How has this individualism affected the local church?

In what way are we breaking with the spirit of individualism that marks life in the West, and instead, taking Jesus' prayer in John 17 seriously?

In what ways are we tied together in vital fellowship with other churches?

Do we share in a basic common agreement, regular lively fellowship, training of laborers, and in missionary endeavors with any other churches?

How will it work out in the long term if we largely stand alone as a local church? If we are largely independent, are we willing to pursue closer relationships and accountability with other churches?

We live in a day in which division, strife, and offenses have often replaced the spirit of peace, unity, real fellowship, and non-resistance even in our Anabaptist churches. In what specific ways can we reprogram the minds and hearts of our people to embrace a life of reconciliation, peace and committed fellowship? (Ephesians 2:13-22; 3:9-11).

Fellowship doesn't just happen, it takes action and must be pursued, so what purposeful values and activities can we practice that will help build a community of peace and fellowship that all can see?

It is important to be clear about these questions regarding decision making, role expectations, membership, and fellowship agreements because they relate to the practical functioning of the church. When there is not clarity, the operation and life of the church will be hindered and there will be a cloud of discouragement?

Making Disciples: The Job of the Church

What are we doing to make kingdom disciples?

Do we as a church understand the two different views of discipleship outlined in this book?

A manufacturer must envision the end product before he sets up his factory, likewise, the disciple-making church must have a vision of what a perfected disciple will look like. *What vision and understanding do we want him to have? What attitudes, relationships, and purpose will mark his life?*

If making disciples that know God's will and do it is the job of the church, then what steps will we take to evaluate how well we are doing this and to make action plans?

Are we purposefully making disciples from the cradle to the grave, or is our approach to disciple making casual and arbitrary?

How would we define our method of cradle-to-the-grave discipling and catechism? Does it work? What results are we producing? Is it thorough and systematic enough?

How could we as a church more effectively make disciples and pass on the faith to the next generation?

Do we know what we are trying to pass on?

How well are we communicating and passing on the big picture of Christianity?

What is our vision, purpose, or reason for existence as a church?

Do our people know what our vision is? Is it obvious to observers that we have one?

Does all that we do prepare and enable people to fulfill our kingdom purpose?

Are our children and young people growing up learning to think biblically?

Do they have ownership of what we as a church teach? Do they know why we do what we do?

How are we equipping dads, moms, and families to make disciples? How could we do this better?

Are our sisters being nurtured and instructed? Do we have and release "Titus Two" women to teach the younger women? Do the older women know what to teach the younger, or is it just their own ideas?

The Mission of the Church

Every business has a general objective. It might exist to serve humanity or to provide for the family. Businesses also have specific objectives, like making garden sheds. The objective may be even more detailed—to make quality sheds, economic sheds, portable sheds, or sheds that can be dismantled. To be successful, a business has to have more than a general objective, and to be faithful, a church also must have a purposeful strategy and plan to spread the kingdom life and message.

What is our purpose and mission as a church? Do we have a clear mission?

Jesus, His disciples, and the apostle Paul systematically took the Gospel of the kingdom to every place. Who today will follow their example, and take the Gospel purposefully to other places? Who is preparing these laborers? Who is sending and supporting them?

Do we have such a plan, or is all our mission activity spontaneous? What steps will we take to implement an action plan for spreading the Gospel as a congregation or group of congregations? When will we start making this plan, and who will be responsible to do so?

Do our children, young people, and families anticipate special opportunities for outreach? (If missions is mainly something that happens outside our area, and outside the local church, then we are teaching our people that it is not really important.)

What is our church's local field of active service/mission? Is it local town witness, urban outreach, tract distribution, door-to-door, prison, elderly, or tent evangelism, etc.?

What foreign field are we as a church praying for and involved in?

Are we as a church excited about the Christian life and the opportunities for kingdom advance, or are we overburdened and feeling it is all too hard? If so, why, and what can we do about it?

What Is the Cost of Commitment?

If we are to take kingdom Christianity and kingdom advance seriously, there will be a cost. What kind of cost do you think there would be for you as a church to live a more purposeful kingdom life?

What are the personal and social hindrances that could keep you as a church from being willing to pay the cost?

Are you willing to pay the cost?

How Do We Nurture Vital Spiritual Life?

Do our people personally experience vital, enriching life and communion with God? Have we asked them?

Faith, revival, life, and passion do not just happen, so what can we do to stimulate our people to deep communion with God?

What can we do in our services to distance ourselves from the casual, spectator Christianity that is seeking to overwhelm us, and demonstrate the vital importance of meaningful worship and a continual connection with God?

Do people meet with God in our services?

Are they ministered to physically, emotionally, and spiritually?

What is Your Understanding of Evangelism and Conversion?

How have we been affected by the "save me" gospel?

How does salvation relate to all of life?

How can we make this clearer in our preaching, evangelism, and in the counseling room?

In leading someone to Christ, how do we ensure that they understand that there is a change of kingdoms?

How do we help them repent, make restitution, and break with the old kingdom?

Do we deal with big issues and expectations before conversion and baptism, or leave that for future discipleship?

Who is doing this well? Could we call them to instruct us about evangelism and counseling?

A Call To Strengthen Our Doctrine of the Church

I have suggested that in this particular period of time God is calling His people to review and refocus their understanding of the doctrine, purpose, and practice of the church. *Does your study of the twelve pillars and the above questions confirm the priority of strengthening your corporate understanding of the church? Will you as a ministry team set definite objectives and make plans to accomplish this? Make a list of the foundational questions and issues that you as a ministry team or brotherhood need to give attention to. Now prioritize the list and plan how you will go about addressing these things.*

Remember, a day of accounting is coming, but in the meantime God has not left us alone. He has given us a job to do, and He has given us the fellowship of the church and of the Holy Spirit.